Playing To a Full House

*The people who make the music
of the Texas Hill Country*

The best *Full House* columns by
Phil Houseal

Introduction

When I finally succumbed to appeals to put my columns into a book, the most difficult task was figuring out which ones to include. Thanks to leeway from editors, my wide interests, and short deadlines, the subject material varies widely.

Fortunately, as I compiled the columns, they fell into a pattern. For this book, I decided to feature the folks who make the music and entertainment that defines the Texas Hill Country. They range from the famous to the "used to be famous" to the "someday will be famous" to the "never ever will be known outside of the Hill Country." Regardless of their level of fame, they all share a trait: they are interesting to me.

I hope they are just as interesting to you.

Contents

Playing to a Full House

Playing for Texas

Contents

Playing from the Hill Country

Playing from the Heart

Foreward

I'm not famous enough to write this foreword.

Or at least that's what Phil Houseal keeps telling me.

I'm no Thomas Michael Riley, Ray Price, or Larry Gatlin, but unlike those fine gentlemen, I've actually read more than a few of Phil's columns.

Having served as his editor for the majority of the eight years he's written *Full House*, I've perused through the good, the bad, and the ugly of the work of Fredericksburg's top columnist.

We haven't always agreed on everything—I won't let him pen the column he's always asking to write about Fredericksburg brothels—but in the end, he trusts me to help guide *Full House* to the next level, while I (guardedly) trust he won't up and make the next column he turns in his last.

The reason Phil is the best columnist in the Texas Hill Country, and among the very best in the state of Texas, is that he cares more about the story than anything else.

He delivers on the stories people want to read because they're the stories he'd want to read himself.

This collection represents the absolute best one of Texas' most unique and charismatic writers has to offer.

Phil began as an entertainment columnist; what he has become is an entertaining columnist.

You don't have to be funny to be entertaining, and that's the difference between good columnists and great columnists.

Sit back, relax and let Phil entertain you in a way few other columnists can.

2013 Matt Ward, Full House Editor
Fredericksburg Standard-Radio Post, Fredericksburg TX

Acknowledgements

For years I dreamed of writing a newspaper column.

I used to submit ideas to area publications, but was ignored or turned down, once with a scathing critique from a respected publisher.

So when Terry and Cathy Collier of the *Fredericksburg Standard-Radio Post* called me in that summer of 2005 to ask me to write an entertainment column, I'm not sure who was more startled when my initial answer was, "No."

The thought of filling a weekly white space was daunting, especially when placed on top of my full time and side jobs, and family commitments. In their kindness and wisdom, they asked me to consider it, and assured me it would be fine if I ever had to skip a week.

So I went home and painstakingly wrote a half dozen sample columns, mainly to reassure myself that I could do it. I went back and timidly handed them in.

Turns out that some 8 years and 500 columns later, I have never missed a column. Sure, some may have been less than book-worthy, but often the ones I feel insecure about are the ones readers love most–a phenomenon I imagine most writers have experienced.

So to Cathy and Terry Collier, thank you for having more confidence in me than I had in myself.

To Ken Esten Cooke, who followed the Colliers as Publisher, thanks for keeping me on.

To my several editors, who inherited me along with writing obituaries and covering school board meetings–thank you for editing with a light touch, while saving me from embarrassing errors (aspiring writers, learn to appreciate editors).

To Matt Ward, who keeps re-inheriting me as his responsibility, for suggesting interesting topics and helping me find that always elusive angle, and especially for holding me to the standard of a "Full House" column.

Finally to all the subjects of my column–thanks for trusting me to share your stories. And for those who have yet to be covered, remember... be patient.

But most of all, be interesting.

Phil Houseal 2013

All photography by Phil Houseal, with the exception of promotional photos provided by Ponty Bone, Ray Price, Georgette Jones, Paul Camfield, and Michael Martin Murphey.
"Philvis" photo by Matt Ward.

Cover Photo Credit: Phil Houseal
Cover Design: Christie Kitchens
www.christiekitchens.com
christiekitchens@gmail.com

Follow Phil Houseal's weekly Full House columns
HillCountryMusic.net
www.fullhouseproductions.net
Facebook: Full House Productions
Fredericksburg Standard-Radio Post

Also by Phil Houseal

Finding Fredericksburg:
A Self-Guided Tour through Historic Fredericksburg, Texas
www.findingfredericksburg.com

Phil Houseal is a writer, educator, musician, and owner of Full House PR, a public relations firm that tells the story of your product, service, or business. Contact him at phil@fullhouseproductions.net.

The Music of the Hill Country
Inaugural Full House column
August 3, 2005

Listen.

That sound you hear is the music of the Hill Country.

This is a column about that music.

My goal is to bend an ear toward the incredible wealth of live music we have access to almost every day of the week, every week of the year.

I plan to share stories of the people who write the music; the people who play the music; and the businesses and organizations that provide a stage for musicians.

There will be stories of famous, successful musicians, and the seasoned professionals playing the club circuit. There will also be stories about the guy singing over the Friday night buffet; the young dreamer writing songs in his bedroom; the retired rancher who picks up his fiddle again. I want to feature the pit musician as well as the conductor of the choir.

All together their voices make the music that is becoming known as the Hill Country sound.

Along the way I hope–with your help–to define "Hill Country music."

My only guide is that I am going to write about what I find of interest. That should not be limiting, as I find most everything in life interesting. The challenge and hope is make readers share that interest.

My hope is that it will encourage you to venture forth and add your voice to music of the Hill Country.

Playing to a Full House

Some of the more recognized artists who've come through or from the Texas Hill Country

Monte Montgomery: Playing with Passion

I wish I could say I recognized the musical brilliance of the 14-year-old boy hanging out at Luckenbach in the 1980s.

When we wannabe musicians gathered under the spreading oak tree to do the traditional "guitar pull," there was often a slight, shy, shaggy-mopped boy sitting just outside the picking circle, playing endless runs up and down his battered acoustic guitar.

I wish I could say he was always welcome. But–truth be known–some of the seasoned pickers groused about the kid who "played too much" when they were trying to sing their precious songs.

Today, Monte Montgomery is a guitar god. Those who grumbled are still playing at Luckenbach for free, and now have to pay to see the kid they wished would go away.

I assume everyone knows Monte Montgomery. He has been named one of The Top 50 All-Time Greatest Guitarists, appeared on *Austin City Limits*, performed for 200,000 at international music festivals, and has a guitar designed and named for him by Alvarez.

Twenty-five years after those afternoons in Luckenbach, I had one question for Monte: Where did he get his style? He created a sound that did not exist before, that is unlike any I've heard. Not pop, not blues, not rock, not country, not Americana–it's blazing, blistering Monte. I asked him that question.

He smiled, then replied slyly, "Maybe I just copy people and disguise it better."

He went on. "I have influences like everybody–I just try to get them across in a way that is not so apparent. I soak up everything that appeals to me. It's not something I set out to do, it is just an evolution of music over the years, it's just the way it came out."

Turns out we pickers in the 1980s did influence the young Montgomery, but not in the way we imagined.

"I remember playing picking up my first chords and watching you guys and saying what chord was that?" he said. "There was a time I moved up to the level you guys were at, and kind of kept moving."

"Yeah," I interrupted, "like at age 12."

He laughed, but didn't disagree. "I didn't think much of it at the time. I had the ability to pick it up quick."

It was around that time that he realized playing the guitar was what he was meant to do.

"I think I was predestined to do what I do, I really do," he said. "I believe that God touched me and chose me to do what I do."

Even the fact that Monte did not attend high school played a part in pointing him to where he is today.

"There's a reason I didn't go to high school and haven't really needed high school. That allowed me all the extra time to play and work on my craft. I think all those factors played an integral part in getting me where I'm at."

Even with divine guidance, the arc of Monte's life has not been all harmony and light. His most recent and painful tragedy was the violent loss of his daughter in March. Like everything in his life, he found a way to use that as part of his passion.

"I don't see a point in trying to avoid letting those things inspire me, even though they might be dark things," he said. "It is really my therapy, it's my release. It doesn't matter what is going on in my life, when I get up on stage it all melts away. It hasn't been easy, but it's never occurred to me to not do what I do; it's a part of me."

Then he said something we all should have recognized back when he was 14.

"To me, I'm not performing. I do what I do because I love what I do."

Dec 23, 2009

Ray Price: Visit With A Legend
Part I

So what do you ask a legend?

If you could interview country music superstar Ray Price, what would you say?

This gave me considerable pause when Gene Wolf of Sharity Productions arranged a phone interview in anticipation of Price's Christmas concert at Cailloux Theater in Kerrville.

After all, what question can you ask that he hasn't answered a hundred times?

Turns out, you don't have to ask him anything. You just visit with him.

When Ray Price came on the phone, it felt as if I was sitting at a small table in a small bar in a small town, and Mr. Price just happened to walk in.

That small-town tavern in my mind was real. It was the place where I was introduced to Ray Price through his music. When I was 19 years old, I played with Frankie Lee and the Swingmasters. Frankie Lee's "go to" singer was Ray Price. I didn't realize that during those cold, cold Saturday nights in Iowa I was playing a future catalog of country classic: *Cold, Cold Heart; For the Good Times; Release Me; Crazy Arms; City Lights*; and on and on.

When I finally got to talk to Price in person, I learned about the man behind those songs.

I asked how his singing voice at age 86 stays so clean and sincere. "I honestly think I sing better than ever," he said with a laugh. "I might be fooling myself, but I have learned different things through the years about my voice. I have always studied my voice. It's my instrument. I guess I was born with it. By age 5 or 6, I sang all the time on the farm. It was just a natural thing."

I learned that while he always wanted to be a singer, he actually started off studying to be a veterinarian. His music career was practically an accident.

"For kicks I would get up to sing in an East Dallas cafe," he recalled of his college years. "They would get people out of the audience to sing. I liked it, and would go out there."

One day a guitar player asked Price to come with him to sing a couple of his songs for a music publisher. "I thought, well, I'll go ahead. There's nothing wrong with helping somebody out."

During a break in the recording at the radio station, Price sang a couple of songs. They stopped him and asked if he could come back the next day. Price said, sure. The next day the owner of a Nashville record label signed him to a contract. "That's when I discovered what I really like to do," Price said with a chuckle. So long, vet school.

I learned that at age 86, Ray Price is having the time of his life.

"I'm enjoying it more than I did before," he said. "Now that I can succeed in doing what I want to with my voice. Until I lose my vocal chords, I'm going to continue doing it."

That's probably not an issue. Because, while he has "a lot of older fans," younger fans are discovering him. I know this first hand, because when I took my 15-year-old daughter to his spring concert, I expected her to be indifferent. Instead, she told me, "I really love that guy. I didn't realize I would recognize all those songs." She became a fan.

"Well, there are not hordes of them," he said of his followers under age 30, "but they are coming more and more all the time. I like to think it's because our music is just good music. It's not like other music that claims it is country music. I think more needs to be done to expose the world to better classes of music than bunches of people screaming and jumping up and down." He paused, then added, "Though I guess that would be all right if you were standing on a fire."

Nov. 14, 2012

Ray Price with Guich Koock

Ray Price: Visit With A Legend
Part II: Shuffles & Strings

When I first came to Texas, I was expected to learn a drumming style called the "shuffle beat." I had never heard or seen the two-step, let alone been inside a real dance hall. That beat, my band mates patiently explained, was the "shuffle" beat.

Guess what? Ray Price invented it–both the word and the rhythm.

"Guilty," Price said when I asked him. "I invented the word 'shuffle beat.'"

It happened at the session when they were recording *Crazy Arms*. The drummer was legendary Nashville studio musician Buddy Harman.

"I said, Buddy, can you play me a shuffle beat on the drums? He looked at me as if I was on another planet. I said, I'd like to see if we could play a shuffle. Do it with a 4/4 beat." Buddy fooled around and finally nailed it. "Thank God it worked!"

Price admitted getting the idea while playing in honky-tonks. "I kind of heard it when I played a dance," he said. "When playing music, if you all of a sudden stop, you hear feet shuffling on the floor. And it worked."

Price also gets credit for introducing another innovation to standard country music. This one gets a stronger and more divided response.

Strings.

Price explained that he first heard strings while working on a faith album with Anita Kerr. He liked the sound of it and figured he could get away with adding strings to his faith songs, since "they didn't play a lot of it on the radio."

But further down the line, he heard Tex Ritter, Stan Kenton, and Eddy Arnold experiment with orchestral arrangements.

"By that time I was ready for it," he said. So when he went in to record *Danny Boy*, he asked if he could use 17 strings players. The producer said, absolutely.

Unfortunately, the traditionalists in Nashville gave him heat over it. So much heat, that Price decided to move back to Texas. So, in a way, was Price the original "outlaw?"

"Well, one of them," he admitted. "They said I had gone 'pop,' which wasn't the case at all. So I got me a 22-piece orchestra and hit the road." He chuckled. "It scared people to death when I played. They hadn't seen nothing like that. God bless them, they stayed with it and gave me all the credit."

Of course after six decades of singing it, Ray Price is country music. Even he admits it.

"If I stand on my head and sing the Star Spangled Banner backwards, they'll say it's country music," Price said. "I try to do it my way. Everything so far has succeeded."

I wanted to ask about Kris Kristofferson, and Willie Nelson, and Johnny Bush, but Price was more interested in letting his fans know he is still recording. He is at this moment in a recording studio working on a new CD of love songs. "This is going to be for ladies only," he said. "Now may be a good time to do this, because country music needs all the help it can get."

Price remembers fondly his concert in Kerrville earlier in the year. "It was great," he said. "Seems they really enjoyed the show.

And he wants everyone to come out again and "see me while you can," he laughed. "It might be the last time." Not that he plans to quit touring. Price battled cancer, and professes to have it under control. "I am ready and raring to go," he said. "Tell your readers that we are back swinging!"

Nov. 21, 2012

Original drummer John Ike Walton with iconic logo

Still on the 13th Floor

Unless you were growing up in south Texas in the late 1960s, you might have missed the 13th Floor Elevators.

I did.

Until the day John Ike Walton walked in and handed me the video *You're Gonna Miss Me*.

Wow.

I was amazed to learn that a bunch of plain-talking boys from the Texas hill country created the seminal sound for a generation of rock and roll bands.

It takes a book to recount the history of the band (and one has been written–*Eye Mind: The Saga of Roky Erickson and The 13th Floor Elevators* by Paul Drummond). But in a capsule, the 13th Floor Elevators started in Kerrville as The Lingsmen in 1965. In addition to Walton on drums, the band included fellow Kerrville resident Ronnie Leatherman on bass, and Stacy Sutherland on guitar. They added singer/songwriter Roky Erickson, along with their signature "electric jug" player Tommy Hall, and became 13th Floor Elevators.

Within months after forming, the Elevators had a Billboard chart hit (*You're Gonna Miss Me*) and went on a west coast tour. They played The Avalon and The Fillmore. Among their followers were members and future members of the Grateful Dead, Steppenwolf, Moby Grape, and ZZ Top.

Walton and his wife Alice graciously invited me to spend an afternoon at their Hill Country hideaway (in a future column I will write about their music instrument business).

Walton has a philosophical take on the band's musical influence. "Our music was not their inspiration since those other bands don't sound like us," he explained. "No, our success drove them–the fact we were out of Texas and we were the first Texas band to play *American Bandstand*. We were the spark that kept them going."

(It was on *Bandstand* that Hall famously replied to Dick Clark's query as to who was head man of the group, with, "Well, we're all heads." Cut to commercial.)

Fredericksburg native Jimmy Reichenau considers himself the band's biggest fan. Too young to hear them live in 1966, he remembers seeing the Elevators on *American Bandstand* and listening to his sister's records.

"When I heard them on record I flipped out," he said, the excitement still evident in his voice. "Because nobody ever played anything like that. I was amazed at their talent. Then there was that whole psychedelic sound."

The Elevators coined the term "psychedelic rock" and it is not surprising. While Walton and Leatherman disavowed the drug use, drugs did figure highly in the Elevators approach to music. Others in the band didn't play a gig without tripping on a cocktail of acid, speed, grass, and who knows what else. That intense use–along with the usual tragic elements of early rock bands–bad deals with record companies and squabbles among members–led to a brilliant but brief time in the spotlight. Walton and Leatherman left the band in July 1967, and the Elevators disbanded when Roky Erickson committed himself to a mental hospital in 1969.

Forty years on, the Elevators continue to influence artists and are being rediscovered by a new generation. Walton recently went into a music store, where a 30-year-old clerk noticed his 13th Floor Elevators T-shirt. "Hey, I've heard of you guys," the young man said, then asked Walton, "Weren't you before Emerson, Lake, and Palmer?"

Walton laughed. "Heck, we were before dirt."

Since leaving the Elevators, Walton has continued to play music, drumming with Roger Miller, Doug Kershaw, and Ray Price. He works as a carpenter, teaches guitar and banjo, and builds and sells kalimbas and African drums. Walton recently started performing Elevators classics with the John Ike Walton Revival.

Fan Reichenau has built a relationship with Walton, and still believes in the magic of the Elevators.

"There are good people, great people, and gifted people," said Reichenau, who once booked the Elevators into the Fredericksburg VFW Hall ("George Strait used to come hear us there," Walton remembered, "back when he had long hair."). "Those guys were gifted. Like a lot of people in the world, they should be millionaires. Luck didn't happen; they self-destructed. But I think their music is awesome."

So how do we reconcile where we are compared to where we might have been? Would any of us have done anything differently than John Ike Walton did?

"You just went with what you thought you should do at the time," Walton said in his plainspoken manner. "LSD has been described as a drug that puts people on a quest for introspection. You are supposed to arrive at a place where you have a grip on everything. I still haven't figured all this out."

"I'm still on the 13th floor."

March 4, 2009

You Raise Me Up

I first heard acclaimed tenor Donald Braswell singing in a vineyard near Fredericksburg on November 7, 2007. I–along with many of you–next heard Donald Braswell in the summer of 2008 on the national television program *America's Got Talent*.

That November evening at Torre di Pietra, Braswell joined San Antonio tenors William Chapman and Tim Birt to electrify a local audience with a tribute to Luciano Pavarotti, famed Italian tenor who died that year.

But during that evening on television, Braswell did not electrify anyone at first. During the beginning of *You Raise Me Up*, the studio audience hooted to run the Boerne native off the stage. It was like the *Gong Show*. But by the time he hit that second refrain, the audience turned, and actually ended up giving him a standing ovation.

If that is all you know, the story is heartwarming. The earnest young man, after a touring career as an opera singer, wins over a tough audience.

But Braswell's story becomes miraculous when you learn that in 1995 he was involved in a car accident that damaged his throat. Doctors told him not only would he never sing, he might not be able to speak normally. Braswell set out to rehabilitate his instrument, and returned to singing, culminating in his emotional turn on the popular TV show (he finished in 4th place, by the way). He now has resumed his touring and singing.

That scene on television reflects something deeper in Braswell's life.

"As a professional opera singer, I had an amazing amount of attention poured on me–people telling me I was the greatest thing since sliced bread," he said. "When you are young and receive all that attention, you start to believe it. After the accident, I had a divine experience. I realized this isn't about me; it is about things so much more important. There is so much all of us can do with our gifts if used right."

During his second shot at fame, Braswell is using his gift to "try to transform people's lives." One transformation is to bring the general audience to the beauty and power of the classical arts.

It may surprise fans to hear Braswell say that he does not consider what he does now as opera.

"The reality of what I do now is contemporary commercial, an art form that appeals to a larger audience than opera would," he explained. "Our goal as artists is to introduce classical arts to an audience in a way not to push them away from it."

Braswell notes that artists such as Andrea Boccelli and Josh Grobin are taking genres of music that were traditionally pop culture–Broadway, early rock, even R&B–adding orchestration, and taking them into the classical field. That is making people look at music differently.

"They can take that and go on to more traditional forms of classical music," he said, adding, "But we will never be in a place where classical music is a pure art form, not in this country, not with a mass audience."

But Braswell's destiny goes beyond saving the classical music industry.

"As an artist, my goal is to inspire people to reach deep in themselves, to cure ills for themselves," he said. "I have had tremendous response to what I have done as an artist. The TV show did expose obstacles I had to overcome in my life. But we all have terrible obstacles in life–relationships, lawsuits, death, illness. It's OK if you have fall-en, and fallen 100 times. The goal is you don't give up and you get back on. Your dream may not come out the way you thought, but you will have results."

"Getting back on is the most important thing."
June 24, 2009

Radio Personality "Big G," Larry Gatlin, Kinky Friedman

Will the Real Larry Gatlin
Please Sit Down?

When promoter Gene Wolf asked if I wanted to interview Larry Gatlin before his upcoming Hill Country show, I said yes. I had a question I'd been waiting 30 years to ask him.

So when the phone rang and I heard, "Phil, this is Larry Gatlin. How are you?" I launched into it.

In one of my former lives, I was playing banjo (badly) in a band in Eldon, Iowa, famous for being home of the farmhouse behind the dour couple in Grant Wood's *American Gothic*.

One night at band rehearsal, a band member stormed in and said, "Last night I heard Larry Gatlin on *The Tonight Show* saying that nobody knew how to write a good song." He was upset. "Well, I'm going to prove to him that I can write just as good a song as he can."

The fact that I can't remember his name, and that no one else has heard of this guy, proves that Larry Gatlin was right. But I had to ask Gatlin: Did you really say that?

He laughed and told me the full story.

"Well first of all, your friend put a little hair on that story," Gatlin said in his West Texas drawl. "I don't have anything against people trying to write a song. But here's what I used to do on *The Tonight Show*."

17

Gatlin related how Johnny Carson was a fan of songwriters. In fact, Carson hearing Gatlin's story song *Penny Annie* was the reason Gatlin was invited to be a guest.

The first time the young Gatlin sat down next to the famous television host, Carson didn't ask any of the questions the producers had prepared. Carson instead wanted to talk about writing songs.

"He said, Larry, people are always trying to tell me jokes. I'm sure they are always trying to sing songs to you. So I told him about the night one good old boy came up after a concert and wanted me to listen to one of his songs. I asked, is it as good as those 15 I just sang? He said no. So I said, why would I want to sing it?"

To demonstrate, Gatlin crooned one of the worst tunes that anyone had ever submitted to his publishing company. He sang it to me over the phone:

Oh honey won't you quit your job
Oh honey won't you quit your job
You went to lunch
With your boss
When you got back
There was still a sandwich in your sack

It got such a reaction from the comic master, Carson did a "spit take across the desk."

"I'm not saying people can't write a song," Gatlin said. "When I lead a writing workshop, I explain that you all are songwriters. But I'll bet you aren't all song craftsmen. There is only one in here, and that's me. But let me help nudge you gently along that path to beginning to learn the art and craft of writing songs."

There is no doubt about Gatlin's ability at crafting a song. His hits include *Broken Lady, All the Gold in California, Houston (Means I'm One Day Closer to You), She Used to Be Somebody's Baby*, and *Talkin' to the Moon*. As a solo artist, and with his brothers Rudy and Steve, Larry Gatlin had 33 Top 40 hits mostly through the 70s and 80s.

As someone who is "in love with the English language," he continues to hone his craft, just as his songwriting heroes did.

"Kris Kristofferson, Roger Miller, Willie Nelson, Mickey Newberry, and John Cash... those were wordsmiths," he said. "None of them were born writers, but they got better as they went along."

Gatlin is so absorbed in developing as a song crafter, he surprised me by revealing he would have written one of his hits differently today.

There's the line in *I Don't Want To Cry* where Larry Gatlin sings,

"Lay back down and love me, and leave the leaving, 'til later on."
Since the lyric is "lay back down," he now believes the melody could
have gone down in pitch instead of rising as originally written. He
sings to demonstrate how it changes the feel and better fits the lyric.
Of course, it still sounds like a hit.

"Without question, the words should drive the melody," he said. "I
call it melody matching. If you have a very plaintive part in your song,
I think it should be on a minor chord, or an augmented or diminished.
It adds a little different color. The melody should always be slave to
the lyrics."

Again he demonstrates with a song. But this is one from slightly
outside his repertoire.

Beethoven.

"How about my favorite Beethoven symphony? I love the 9th!" he
announced, then robustly began singing the familiar tune–in German,
no less. "That is *Ode to Joy*. It is joyful, and it's big, and it is up in a
major key. What if he had done this like he did with his 5th symphony?" Gatlin then sang the famous minor four-note refrain da-da-da-
dah. "Oh-am-I-happy? No, no, no! That is the method to my madness."

Actually I had a second question I wanted to ask Larry Gatlin.

It was in line with his belief that while anyone can be a songwriter,
only a dedicated few earn the designation of song crafter.

The question was this: There are literally thousands of talented singers and musicians out there struggling to reach success in the music
industry. Why do certain ones make it? What do they have that sepa-
rates them from the herd? What is "it?"

He agrees there is an "it."

"You can't fix it in the mix," he explained. "You can overdub all the
instruments and all the voices, but you can't overdub the feel. Willie
Nelson is not a classical singer; he is a song stylist."

Then he mentioned his long and close relationship to Johnny Cash.

"Here is the answer to your question: John Cash never in his life
ever adorned a song to make it about him. It was about telling the
story, about coming up organically from the earth."

As an example, Gatlin sang one of Cash's hits–*One Piece At A Time*.

"Every old boy can identify with that song. One interviewer asked
me what I thought about putting John Cash on a stamp. I said as far as
I'm concerned, you could put John Cash on the flag."

Guests at the Gatlin show will hear more tidbits like this, along with
Gatlin's personal recollections of his interactions with such stars such
as Kristofferson, Jimmie Dean, Dottie West, and Elvis Presley. On
stage will be Larry Gatlin and one guitar player.

"I'm working on a show I call 'will the real Larry Gatlin please sit down,' because when I first started here in Nashville I just sat down on a stool and did it. That's what I'm going to be doing that night."

Even though Gatlin famously holds strong opinions, you won't hear them at his show.

"People still want to hear me sing, thank God," he said. "The audience does not come to be preached to; they do not come for politics. You will get the hits, and you will get some humor, and I pick on myself as much as anyone else. It's all in good fun."

I can vouch for that. As I end our call, I hear him singing:

Oh honey won't you quit your job...

July 3, 2012

Accordion According to Bone

Ponty Bone has drawn from rock, Cajun, and Zydeco to create his unique accordion sound, which he will feature with his band, the Squeeze Tones.

With apologies to Barbara Mandrell, Ponty Bone was "accordion" when the accordion wasn't cool.

In fact, it's fair to say Ponty Bone was the man who made the much-maligned instrument hip. Bone took the accordion from *Lady of Spain* fame to being the central instrument in the whole cajun, zydeco, folk, roots sound that is now wildly popular.

"Yeah, I started out playing the stuff," Bone admitted when I asked him about his early training. "I played standard sheet music when I took lessons from age 5 to 12. I had to have the lesson prepared or face the consequences. But it was that stuff that gave me technique and theory. I've always been thankful that I know about that.

"But," he laughed, "like most musicians, I don't let it get in the way of playing."

The way Ponty Bone plays is his own creation. And it almost didn't happen.

"At the age of 12 I told my dad I wanted to quit accordion," he said. "I had already determined that the accordion wasn't cool."

But it was the 1950s, and Bone started to discover some great music on the radio–Fats Domino, Little Richard, Chuck Berry.

"I could figure out how to play it on accordion and this was interesting to me. It didn't seem to be a career option, but it kept my musical interest alive."

At age 18, Bone discovered Louisiana music, and started incorporating Cajun and Zydeco into his sound. He said "adios" to the *Lady of Spain* for good.

"This new stuff sounded excellent, and I didn't care what anybody thought," he said. "I started playing it at parties, and people encouraged me to keep on doing it."

Bone never cared much about being popular. That freed him up to explore many side trails in the music world. In fact, he seems to use his rebel image as inspiration.

"I've always lived life as if I was the subject of a novel," he said. "It's a novel about a guy with artistic pursuits, not a guy selling shows."

That approach makes it hard to categorize Bone's music: the music industry is not sure where to put him. It tried Americana, but the latest article I read labeled him as folk rock. It seems to me Bone IS a genre.

"I am," he said. "But there is nobody else in it."

That doesn't bother him, either.

"Life might be easier if there were a category for me, and I could say I was routinely played on a radio station that promoted my genre. Whether I planned it or it happened that way, I'm stuck with it and it doesn't hold me back."

Whatever label you stick on his sound, it goes great with crawfish. Wherever Bone plays, his music comes with a helping of that Louisiana treat.

"That all started when I carried crawfish and Texas wine to Canada one time," he explained. "A bunch of us put on a crawfish party every night we played. The Canadians went from 'how do you eat these things' to everybody going through a pound of it. Now, it sort of makes an appearance at a lot of my shows."

Sixty years after picking up the accordion, Bone still enjoys sharing his style with the world.

"I do it because I can," he said. "I'm still able to really cut loose on that thing. It's good medicine for me and people seem to love it. I've tried lot of different things in life, but when it's all said and done, this is it."

May 23, 2007

Planet Fredericksburg:
John Andrew Parks III

Another musician just landed on Planet Fredericksburg. You may not have heard of John Andrew Parks III, but you probably heard a song he wrote. It was a groundbreaking number called "Planet Texas" that was a Top 40 hit recorded by Kenny Rogers in 1989.

After spending a career in places like Los Angeles and New York, Parks yearned for a bit of peace where he could continue his work in the music production business. The Dallas native spent months driving around the hill country. Fredericksburg fit.

"I could be looking at graffiti in LA or I could be in Fredericksburg," he remembered thinking. "I really liked this place. I felt it is kind of like Mayberry, yet close to Austin and with a really strong music scene."

Thanks to computer technology, the producer-singer-songwriter can access his network of musicians across the country. "With digital tools I don't really need to be anywhere, so I might as well be someplace I like," he said.

When not in the studio, Parks plays the coffeehouse and house concert circuit, and has seen his performing persona evolve over his 30 years in the business.

"I'd describe my style as Roy Orbison meets Will Rogers," he said. "I do a lot of story songs. I got into telling stories on stage, and the audience got so they responded to that."

The song *Planet Texas* is the ultimate story song. The style was so unexpected in the 1980s, none of Parks' friends expected it to get recorded, let alone become a hit.

"When I wrote Planet Texas, people said, 'no way–that's too far out there.' But that was the first song that made me money."

So I asked 'em as they pulled their reins towards the settin' sun
I said, "Before you go, I'd like to know, just where you boys come from?"
Well they opened up a star chart and said, Right here where this 'X' is
*It's the biggest place in Outer Space, the planet known as Texas"**

Parks seems to revel in his rebel approach inside a sometimes staid industry. With his technical tools and creative attitude, he is proud to go his own way.

"Record companies want consistency in the recorded product," he explained. "If you come along and are way off what was there, they don't know what to do with it. But you are an artist–what you are supposed to do is explore those new worlds. That's the real estate I own–I can do it whatever way I want."

Welcome to Planet Fredericksburg.
Jan 9, 2008

*"Planet Texas" copyright 1986 by Hilalou Publishing Company

Jeneé: Stepping into the Spotlight

Music history is replete with stories of backup band members who stepped up to become headliners in their own right:
- Willie Nelson first played bass for Ray Price
- Waylon Jennings was one of Buddy Holly's Crickets
- Faith Hill was discovered singing backup in a cafe

This weekend, you can watch and listen as another talented backup musician takes one of her first steps into the spotlight.

Jeneé Fleenor is the featured guest artist at The Rockbox Theater. In addition to being the first chance for local folks to hear her, it is her first trip to Fredericksburg. But this ain't her first rodeo.

Before joining McBride, Jeneé (rhymes with Reneé) toured with country star Terri Clark for seven years, appeared on the Grand Ol' Opry several times, and played on TV shows such as Good Morning America, The View, and the CMA Awards. For the past year she has backed up Martina McBride on vocals, mandolin, and mostly fiddle. It was never her goal to be "the artist."

"If you would have asked me 10 years ago to front a band as an artist, my answer would have been no," the Arkansas native confessed. "I don't know if being in Nashville had anything to do with it, but I got bitten by the bug."

Although she has played violin since age 3, she picked up the guitar only a few years ago so it would be easier to accompany herself. As she dutifully learned her first three chords, she discovered it opened up a whole new world of songwriting.... with a bullet. Jeneé co-wrote the song *I Am Strong* which has been sung by Dolly Parton and is on The Grascals #1 Billboard Bluegrass album.

"I think the artist thing opened up for me when I started songwriting. I thought, man, I really want to sing these songs that I write."

In fact, it is Jeneé's quest to step to the front of the stage that brought her to Fredericksburg's Rockbox Theater.

"Any opportunity to do my own thing, I want to branch out and do that now," she said. "*I Am Strong* was a blessing, and is helping me write more. I didn't want to wait 10 years and wonder why I didn't do the artist thing."

At the popular Fredericksburg show venue, Jeneé plans to perform songs off her new EP release, including her version of *I Am Strong*. Of course no fiddler can get off the stage in Texas without playing *Orange Blossom Special*. Jeneé spits out her own interpretation of this fiddle staple, which sometimes includes snippets of theme songs from old TV shows.

Playing with arguably the top female country artist currently performing has been an adventure–one she still doesn't quite believe.

"I got a call from Martina's bandleader asking if I wanted this gig. I thought, are you kidding?"

Her first big show was in her home state of Arkansas, a venue she had never done with a headliner. She made her entrance rising up through the stage floor, and had a big solo.

"I was a little freaked out," she laughed. "My family was there; it was amazing. I called the bandleader after the show to make sure I really had the gig!"

She did.

As much adrenaline as she produces playing music, her true love is writing music.

"I love songwriting–it is more challenging for me than just playing fiddle," she said. "Playing fiddle comes easy–it flows from me. But songwriting is work."

Her first hit was "one of those rare songs that fell out of sky–it was God-inspired."

But she knows that most songs take a longer time to finish.

"When I first started I thought you sat down and whatever came out was the song," she said. "I had a lot of crappy songs. When I started writing with Nashville songwriters, I picked up on the art of it. I love working towards it."

Then she said something that applies to songs, careers, and life:

"You know when it's right."

Feb 23, 2011

Drummer Durawa

Over his 50-year career, Ernie Durawa has played drums for such music legends as the Texas Tornados, Doug Sahm, Freddy Fender, Flaco Jimenez, and Delbert McClinton.

But given his druthers, Durawa would play Latin Jazz.

That's what he did one weekend at the Roots Music concert at the Pioneer Museum.

I managed to stick a recorder in his face for a few minutes before his set. As one drummer to another, I wanted to talk about the art of drumming–not the glamour of gigs.

Durawa–who will soon turn 70–has been drumming since he was 11. He described it as "just a passion" that he has followed ever since.

The San Antonio native trained under legendary drumming teacher Roy C. Knapp, who taught him technique.

"He told me to practice single strokes, and double strokes, both right-handed and left-handed. He said to me the whole secret to playing drums is having control of single strokes and double strokes and then building up the left hand."

Like all drummers, his evolution as a musician has included shedding instruments. "Yeah, I used to use a lot more equipment," he said. "I got tired of carrying it around. Then again, the kind of gigs I'm doing don't call for all that stuff. This band here, I use a basic set."

"This band" is Los Jazz Vatos, the group he brought to Roots. The band features a horn section, and they play polkas, blues, Latin, soul, and swing. They play salsa, but it "is really not a salsa band," according to Durawa. "This is jazz with a Latin feel. It is a whole other style of playing, and it just feels good to me." Sometimes he adds in another percussion player, which opens up even more rhythmic possibilities.

Coming off a two-hour polka gig myself, I had to ask Durawa about the boredom of playing drums for 50 years. By definition, drumming is keeping the beat. All the other players in a band get to switch between rhythm and lead. They can even stop playing in the middle of a song to sip a beer, and the song won't fall apart. Drummers can't quit until the final note.

That's not an issue for Durawa.

"I have to be playing with different people all the time," he explained, "so I do not get into a boring situation. Most of the time I play with the Tornados, and we play the same tunes for the last 20 years over and over. Sometimes it becomes automatic pilot, but at the same time, we play for huge crowds, so the energy they are giving to you is going back and forth. It just feels good to play that stuff, and it just keeps you going."

Durawa excels at all styles. Still, he would choose that classic format of piano, bass, and drums: the jazz trio.

He did that in Chicago. Setting aside for the moment that the gig happened to be at The Playboy Club, his satisfaction came from the music.

"I just loved it," he said. "I love jazz, and deep inside my heart I always have. Jazz makes me think; makes me use my head. It's not just 'boom chuck, boom chuck, boom chuck.' That can get you bored. Jazz is creative music."

Amazingly, Durawa – the most in-demand drummer in the Austin area – still works the road. Hard. In the single week following his Fredericksburg show, he was off to Lubbock, El Paso, and New Mexico, after a Sunday gig at the Bob Bullock Museum in Austin where the Tornados were being honored with a Grammy display.

And why not? He sees no reason to quit.

"Hey... it's all I know how to do."

One more thing:

While researching the list of musicians Durawa had played with, I came across a name that surprised me: George Gobel. For youngsters, Gobel was a TV personality/ comedian/ pitchman in the 50s and 60s known as "Lonesome George." He played ukulele, and Durawa was his drummer. "We traveled around in a Lincoln Town car," Durawa recalled. "At shows, he'd introduce me this way – 'And on drums over here is my son from my first wife in Tijuana.'"

May 30, 2012

Touched by Angels and Idols

When recent Rockbox Theater guest artist Rick Elias told Creative Director Russ Hearn they might enjoy having Regie Hamm play, Hearn said the same thing I said: "Who?"

Regie Hamm–as everyone will soon know–is a "top drawer talent" who has produced a string of #1 songs in Contemporary Christian music and was the winning songwriter from the hit television show *American Idol*.

"Yeah," laughed Regie Hamm when I called him up, "tell your readers to turn off *American Idol* and come out to see someone who actually wrote the song for it."

It's true. Hamm wrote *Time of My Life*, which won the contest for the 2008 season, became the first release for *American Idol* winner David Cook, and was used by NBC television as its theme song for the 2008 China Olympics. But there is more to the story. Actually there is an entire book–*Angels & Idols*–also written by Hamm.

"If you read his book, you will see what a ride this guy has been on," said Hearn. "I've loved his music, but when I read the book that turned my head around about him. He has been at the top and at the bottom–it is an amazing story."

Angels & Idols details the journey of Hamm and his wife, Yolanda, adopting a little girl in China. Unbeknown to them, the girl they brought home had a severe disability–a mysterious genetic disorder

31

known as Angelman Syndrome. What followed was confusion and heartbreak, round-the-clock care, and heavy medical bills. It was in the spring of 2008, at the absolute bottom, that Regie's wife urged him to enter the *American Idol* songwriting contest.

He poured all his passion into that song, which went on to win and become one of the longest-running chart toppers of all time.

Hearn calls it a "full circle moment."

"Unknown to Regie, his song got picked up by the Olympics in China," Hearn said. "He got a call, and there is his song played as part of ceremonies. That's just his personal story. Those are kind of songs I enjoy listening to because you hear truth in lyrics of things he was living out."

Although Hamm used to live in Texas, this would be his first visit to Fredericksburg and the Hill Country. So why does an international success come play in Fredericksburg?

"A friend of mine–Rick Elias–had played the Rockbox and said, man, you ought to go play there," Hamm explained. "You'll have fun and it will be a great experience." So he contacted them and slotted in from there. "You'd be surprised at the kind of things I do. I'm just a kid from Nashville, happy to be playing. Any day I can be on stage with good musicians, it's a good day."

Hamm helps out those not familiar with his music.

"I get compared to a lot of people. Since I play piano, I am compared to Billy Joel and Elton John, just because I am sitting behind a piano. But I'm too country for pop, and too pop for country. I'm a storyteller first and foremost."

Hamm enjoyed lofty success in the 1990s writing and producing contemporary Christian hits. But he was considered a musical "Jekyll and Hyde."

"I worked days on Christian music, then at night I would play my other songs." The difference? "I was a still a Christian writing them, but I was telling stories in song you probably wouldn't sing from the pulpit."

Bottom line, Hamm was raised by and as a musician, and has been around music his whole life.

"I'm really looking forward to it, man. I love Texas, and I love the people down there. I'm gonna try to rock the Rockbox!"

June 22, 2011

Georgette Jones: 'Til She Can Make It On Her Own

The story of Georgette Jones might best be told in the lyrics of one of Tammy Wynette's hit songs:

I'll need time to get you off my mind

Georgette is, of course, the daughter of George Jones and Tammy Wynette–the King and Queen of country music. Growing up as the offspring of two country music icons can be a "bittersweet" affair, according to Georgette Jones.

"I certainly don't want to sound like whining, because who my parents are is a wonderful thing," Georgette confided during a phone interview. "But it also has drawbacks. It has been difficult only in that for people who book me, their first impulse is to ask me to sing like mom and dad. But it's been fun to discover what I like to write and sing."

She is now putting together personal music projects, ones she promises are more her style of music. What is that style?

"It is kind of difficult to describe my influences," she admits. "I grew up on the traditional country music of people like Vince Gill and Loretta Lynn, which I love. But along the way I also discovered other people who influenced me, like Linda Ronstadt and Bonnie Raitt. They still call me 'country,' but it is more an earthy blues, acoustic sound. It has evolved–it just comes out when I write."

And 'till I get used to losing you, let me keep on using you

But Georgette understands the timeless appeal to fans of her mother and father. That is why during her "tribute" shows, the echo of her mother is uncanny.

"I did not want to sound like mom, because I can't really fill those shoes. So when I'm singing mom's music, it is not a conscious effort to sound like her. But I've listened to her my whole life, so it is embedded in my brain. So when I sing, I'm singing what I heard and what I remember."

It is still an emotional experience to perform her parents' music, especially so soon after losing her father.

"To be honest, for months after my dad passed away, even the fun songs like The Race Is On were still difficult for me to sing. It took me a year and half to even listen to mom's music after losing her. You grow through that, and mom's music is actually therapeutic to me now."

One of those powerful songs that she still cannot perform live is You, Me, and Time, which she wrote and recorded with her famous father.

"I wrote that song with so much love in my heart," she said. "The fact that he not only liked it, but wanted to record it, not as a father, but as an artist, meant the world to me on so many levels. I hope I can share that live one day."

I'll get by, 'til I can make it on my own

Her shows are always a powerful emotional experience, for both the audience and the performer.

"As I said, it is a bittersweet thing. I am able to share that music because I always want people to remember my mom. So I tell different stories, and give some background and history on how a song came about or what it means. It is more than an ordinary tribute–not your typical tribute show. Because my mom was my mom, and my dad was my dad, I am able to share things not normally shared at a tribute concert. It is more personal and meaningful for the people there."

'Til I can make it on my own

"I will always honor my parents, and include their music in my shows. I am in a place now that I wasn't sure I'd ever be in. Things have worked out. I am absolutely thrilled to death to do my own music. Not everyone gets the opportunity to do that."

Nov 27, 2013

Redd Volkaert: Telemaster

If I listed half the famous musicians Redd Volkaert has played with, I'd use up all the words allotted for this column. You could start with Ray Price, Commander Cody, Larry Gatlin, and Bill Monroe and go all the way through George Jones, Dwight Yokum, Kenny Rogers, and Dolly Parton.

Hard to believe when someone first tried to put a guitar in his hands, Volkaert didn't want to take it.

"My dad asked my brother and me if we wanted to play music," remembered Volkaert, who grew up in British Columbia. "I said, no, I'll play soccer. But my brother got a guitar and quit, so I wound up stuck with his old guitar."

Now known as the "Telemaster" for the way he plucks his 1953 Fender Telecaster guitar, Volkaert is a sought-after teacher, sideman, studio/road musician, bandleader, and self-proclaimed "guitar dork."

I've heard him perform locally, and finally caught up with him at Hondo's, where we were able to visit for a few minutes before he had to go on stage (see www.hillcountrymusic.com for a link to that performance).

Volkaert is funny and self-deprecating, as if any kid could pick up a guitar and play like he does. When I asked him when he knew for sure that he was good at playing the guitar and wanted to do it for a living, he deadpanned, "I'm still waiting."

Actually, that revelation came a little earlier in his career. He was 13 and playing guitar in his first club, which happened to be a "clothing

35

optional" venue for certain performers sharing the stage.

"I got to play music, learning from these older musicians, looking at titties? Hell, yeah, this is what I want to do!"

A few years earlier, his musical career looked more tenuous. As a 10-year-old, his guitar teacher "fired" him.

"I wasn't learning to read music," Volkaert confessed. "I was cheating. I'd watch him play, go home and memorize it, then come back and play the lesson for him."

Until one day his teacher busted him.

"I dropped my pick, and when I bent over to pick it up, the teacher had turned the page. So when I came back up, I played the wrong page. He said to my dad, he's got a great ear but he can't read music."

Volkaert later eventually learned to read well enough to stay one lesson ahead of his own guitar students... and to sustain a career playing and recording with the top talent in the country.

In an interesting twist, one of the artists Volkaert liked as a lad was Merle Haggard. Years later Volkaert would tour a hundred shows a year with Haggard. ("When Merle Haggard called and wanted to know if I was interested in working with him, I hesitated... for 3/10ths of a second.")

Now in his 50s, Volkaert still carries that enthusiasm for his chosen instrument. He has his own band–the radically named Redd Volkaert Band–based in Kyle, Texas. Unlike his studio and sideman gigs, this is where he can play all the kinds of music he likes.

"In my own band, I get to play a bit of bluesy stuff. When we play a country song, I can put in a jazzy solo, a blues solo, a country solo, then try to emulate the pedal steel on another solo. To me–if you are feeling a wild hair, let one go."

His jokiness and refusal to take himself seriously reveals a man who is still curious about his instrument and willing to experiment–especially live, on stage.

"I'm always trying to discover what works, mixing and matching styles, trying to come up with stuff nobody else does," he said. "'Live' is always more fun. Playing in the studio is more of a mental challenge, trying to make it perfect. Whereas live it only goes by once, so let's try this. If it doesn't work, who gives a shit."

Backing up the big stars carries a different challenge.

"With some Nashville stars, if you play different than what's on the record, that throws them off," he said. "But that's the job, and if it pays enough, that's what you do."

Aug 21, 2011

A Cowboy Christmas

If you dread the holidays and their treacly traditions, you need to go to one of Michael Martin Murphey's Cowboy Christmas Shows. Spending an evening with the legendary "Singing Cowboy Poet" will cure those holiday blues in ways only a cowboy can.

This ain't Murphey's first rodeo. The Texas native has been a force in the music business since his breakout hit *Wildfire* in 1975. Over four decades he has evolved and grown, turning out progressive country standards including *Carolina In The Pines, What's Forever For, Cosmic Cowboy, Geronimo's Cadillac*, and *Cherokee Fiddle*.

Murphey is a talented performer who brings a surprising depth to any discussion. He studied classical literature, medieval and renaissance history, and literature at UCLA.

When I learned I would be able to interview the artist, I was star struck. It's one thing to talk to the guy who plays the turkey baster, but a star of Murphey's magnitude has been asked all the questions. So I devised a unique interview strategy: I asked friends what they would ask him. They came through with some excellent questions, and some turkeys (What would you do for a Klondike bar?).

So for the rest of this column, I'll step aside and let Michael Martin

Murphey do what he does best–use his own words.

Do you still use fingernail clippers to trim your strings when you change them?

"Ha! That is assuming I change my strings. I just wipe 'em off and play another show."

Why did you start playing?

"My grandpa gave me a ukulele he had brought back from Pearl Harbor when I was 4 years old. He lived in Hawaii but came back to Texas to die. I figured out from that that I loved playing stringed instruments. Next thing you know I'm playing guitar."

You have written and recorded dozens of hits over four decades, and you continue to tour and turn out acclaimed recordings. What is the key to longevity in the music business?

"Work. I am either writing songs, playing songs, or recording songs. It is a three-pronged attack. I have always got more songs around than space for them on an album. I'm always working on some new material. I can tell you this: When the luck comes, you better be ready."

Advice to up and coming songwriters?

"Write, write, write. If you want to be a writer for a living, it is a good idea to study music and literature. If you don't want to read the classics, there is plenty of other stuff to study. That's where you learn phraseology and rhyme schemes. I strongly recommend taking courses in college in poetry and creative writing. I even try to write emails using good form–I don't use shorthand when texting, because that dumbs down the language."

What is the secret to success in the music business?

"It is writing or having access to excellent material. You have to have songs that connect with people. I wouldn't worry about commercial appeal; it is better to have original songs that people connect to. You can test that in a bar or pizza joint, even if only 30 people are sitting there. It is not about you; it's about them. You have to produce an emotional reaction in the people who are listening. The music just adds emotional impact to what you are saying."

On playing in the Hill Country?

"Anybody who doesn't like the Texas Hill Country needs to have their head examined. This drought is just part of the cycle. I am impressed with the way people survive, without a lot of whining. A while back we tried to put together a benefit for ranchers and farmers, and they said, thank you, but no thank you–we don't need charity. Every time someone does a benefit, the government comes in and then next thing you know there are strings attached."

What can people expect at the Cowboy Christmas Show?

"The Cowboy Christmas Show is based on the idea of an old time cowboy remembering back to a simpler time. We go through some of the hit songs, worked in with the Christmas theme. This is a full production show; I don't just stand up and play. We have a campfire on stage, great lighting, and archival video of actual cowboys showing on video backscreens. We are telling a story up there. People are going to be astounded this year at the stuff we are putting on screen. You'll see what ladies wore to the ball in the early 1900s, pictures of old cowboys, and old time trail riders who actually went up the Chisholm Trail."

"My goal is to have any Texan walk out with their chest swelled with pride."

And even if you are not a Texan, after going to the Cowboy Christmas Show, everyone will be a cowboy.

Nov 9, 2011

Playing for Texas

True Texas artists

Erik Hokkanen: Born into Music

I knew Erik Hokkanen was a different sort of musician when he introduced a song by saying, "Here's a little country tune–from the country of Yemen."

The Austin-based artist then took off on a gypsy song in the harmonic minor scale.

The guy first impresses as an insane instrumentalist, equally dazzling on electric guitar and fiddle. But there is something else there. His talent reaches deeper than going pyro on strings. The guy is a born musician. Literally.

"My mom was pregnant with me and was playing the piano," he said. "I was born into music, basically."

He also was led into it by an older brother who shared some eclectic tastes.

"I learned Beatles songs from him when I was 11," Hokkanen said. "Then my brother was playing bluegrass and listening to Irish and folk rock. Then we would practice some old fiddle tune, then next might be a Charlie Parker tune, then Renaissance recorder music. We even listened to Ravel and Debussy."

The young sponge followed a similar journey when it came to choosing a musical instrument. He started playing piano at age 4, then his brother taught him mandolin. Then it was on to sax, which did not satisfy his thirst for musical knowledge, even in 6th grade.

42

"Since it was beginning class, we were given all the long notes–trumpets and flutes got all the melodies," he said. "I became disenchanted with that because I didn't feel there was enough action–I wanted to keep learning and keep playing."

He tried harmonica, then moved to fiddle at the suggestion of his brother. He took lessons both on old-time fiddle tunes and basic classical violin.

Finally, at age 14, Hokkanen got going on guitar. But all the steps leading to that moment helped shape his musical destiny, which goes beyond the instrument.

"The passion is the love for music," he answered. "If you really learn to respect each instrument and what it has to offer, then any instrument can be your instrument of passion."

Hokkanen has become a legend among Austin musicians, and is revered in the Netherlands. But with his eclectic tastes, Hokkanen realizes he may have passed earlier chances for commercial success.

"Back in the late 80s people told me what I was doing was career suicide," he said. "If I'd had a semi-hit with Texas western swing fiddle, then people would want that formula. But I follow my heart the whole way, man. The way I learned is good music is good music."

The music industry may have caught up with Hokkanen. Today there is a market for "a guy who can play a gypsy tune, then a great old fiddle tune, western swing, a Django tune, a surfing tune, then something totally different from all that."

"The job of the musician is to bring out the beauty of the music," he said. "My thing always was to play well."

The self-effacing man seems bemused by his status as a guitar icon. He barely considers himself as a pro.

"I'm still an amateur at heart–I'm still a student. If I have a drop of talent, I think of myself as a brown belt," he laughed, adding, "it's not for me to say I'm great. I'm still in my early 40s and there is a desire to play well. I'm still learning. I've learned a lot but I don't know very much."

Nor does he subscribe to the gunslinger theory of guitar playing. It's always about the music.

"If some guy can do more than me, go for it man," he said. "I don't sweat that–I'm not in competition. That's for other people. For me, it's to play sincerely."

"When you become an artist you become a personality. Your personality is in your playing. I play honestly and sincerely. It's just music. We play good music."

January 23, 2008

Preparing to launch a pie at his father "Icky Twerp," Fredericksburg resident Paul Camfield appears as Mossback (center) during a show commemorating the anniversary of Slam Bang Theater in Fort Worth

Icky Twerp

Kids in the 1950s and 1960s rushed home after school and turned on their televisions to watch shows designed just for them. Depending on where you grew up, your afternoon TV host might have been Dr. Max, Captain Ernie, Buckaroo Bob, or Marshall Jay.

If you lived in Fort Worth, you watched Icky Twerp.

Ichamore Twerpwhistle was the brilliant creation of Bill Camfield, a creative writer who found himself working as promotions manager for independent KTVT-TV (Channel 11) in the 1950s.

Camfield's memory is being kept alive by his son, Paul Camfield of Fredericksburg.

Camfield's Icky Twerp was ahead of his time. Rather than going for some outrageous persona, Camfield made Twerp just slightly off center. He wore an outdated brown suit, and a too-small cowboy hat perched atop a scraggly black wig.

He was a trained actor and voracious reader. His skits often contained references to great literature and obtuse puns (in one skit he dined at the "Toe Main" restaurant).

Like all early children's shows, Slam Bang Theater was a collection of slapstick skits and improvised bits produced to introduce cartoons and Three Stooges shorts. The show featured sidekicks in gorilla suits, hand-drawn scenery on backdrops of brown paper, and lots of pies in the face. It all erupted from Camfield's fertile mind. He was responsible for 2 and 1/2 hours of daily programming five days a week. He created a stable of characters, including Mortimer Moolah, Cosmo the Clown, Hoover the Movie Hound, and Gorgon, who hosted the Nightmare horror movie. Gorgon's signature laugh still haunts his grown son.

Kids loved it. During the later runs of the show, Twerp would draw 5000 youngsters to his public appearances. Heady stuff for the son of a West Texas coal miner. But life behind the scenes was not all posing and pratfalls.

Camfield led a compelling life, torn between talent and tragedy. He grew up dirt poor, and never was able to parlay his TV success into financial security. He lost his wife to suicide, his teenage daughter to a car wreck, and battled and triumphed over personal demons, dying at 62 of brain cancer.

Son Paul Camfield has reached resolution with all sides of the story, and today sees the positive effect his father had on a generation of television viewers. Every day he receives comments from contemporaries who remember the joy and fun Icky Twerp delivered during their growing up years.

"All my emails say the same things, that this meant so much to them and was such a big part of their childhoods." He is also surprised to discover there is interest from today's younger generation. "When we were showing people in their 20s the rushes from the documentary, they were blown away with the reality of it. So this is not just nostalgia for boomers."

Paul was fortunate to be able to grow closer to his father as an adult. He has only one regret, if you could call it that. When I asked him if he had any question he'd like to ask his father, Paul falls uncharacteristically silent. Finally he speaks.

"I would have loved for him to see my kids in their theater and dance performances. When I watched my youngest perform in a play, I was just crying like a baby. If dad had been sitting in the audience that night, he would have been bawling too. It was just beautiful to see that, yes, they do have a little of that in them."

Sept 9, 2009

Denny Hardy: Still blowin'

Denny Hardy played saxophone in Tex Beneke's band, jammed with Al Hirt and Pete Fountain, battled head to head with Boots Randolph, and recorded a hit record with David Lee Roth. Not bad for a farm boy from Missouri who honed his licks in an outhouse.

As a youngster, Hardy wanted to play saxophone so bad that he spent hours practicing in the "outdoor" bathroom.

"Now that's wanting to learn to play!" he laughed as I visited him in his hill country home where he has lived since 1992. Now 77 and dealing with emphysema, Hardy still loves the saxophone and still plays in the Bill Smallwood Orchestra.

In spite of his intoxicating experiences at the pinnacle of the big band and jazz music scene in the 1960s and 70s, for Hardy it was all about the instrument. He decided to pick it up because he "just loved the sound of it."

Hardy actually started playing tenor banjo at the age of five. It was something you did in a musical family. He had seven brothers and sisters, and both his parents were musicians, playing in roadhouses.

But it was not until after he returned from the army at age 20 that he started learning sax. He had tried clarinet, and later learned enough guitar from Don Barber of the Four Freshman to play with jazz groups such as the Mike Kasberg Trio.

But no instrument matched the feeling the saxophone gave him.

"I liked the sound of it. How can I say it? It was just something beautiful. You can express feeling. Other people could tell how you felt by way that you played."

But when Hardy first hit the road in 1954 and was finally playing sax in a real band, he wasn't happy with the way he played.

"I just didn't know how," he said. "I could play melodies, and take stupid, full rides. But I was in the back seat."

That's when a guy name Bill Widdicomb came in to the band. Hardy recalls him as "the best alto sax player I ever heard in my life."

"He took a liking to me, and said he would teach me if I bought the beer."

It took cases of beer and three hours a day five days a week, and that was the easy part.

"Whenever I made a mistake, he'd say you really are good–we might put you in the 8th grade band. It was a real putdown. I was so mad, I was trembling." But it motivated the son of a sharecropper. "I said, you SOB, I'm going to learn to play as good as you do."

Hardy smiled. "Well, I didn't get that good, but I cut it pretty close. In the end, I was thankful he showed me what to do."

The secret is something Hardy never forgot.

"He told me, 'When you play, it's not your horn you are holding, it's your heart. That's not just a piece of brass; you must make it a part of you.'"

Hardy hit some heady heights holding his horn. He played top clubs and for a while worked in Nashville, where he was a sought-after studio musician and sat in the stage band of the popular *Ralph Emery Show*.

Hardy had graduated from the outhouse to the hottest jazz stages in the world. While living in Baton Rouge, he would play his club gig from 10 p.m. to three in the morning, then jump in the car and drive down to New Orleans where he jammed at Louis Prima's club with Al Hirt, Pete Fountain, and Sam Butera until 7 a.m.

"I was young and I stayed up all night. I loved to play," he said, adding, "I wish I could do that now."

Long after his days playing music all night, it seemed the music world wasn't quite through with Hardy's talents. In 1985 he got a call from a music producer in Louisiana asking Hardy if he had heard of the song *I'm Just a Gigolo*.

"I said I played that many, many times with Louis Prima and Sam Butera. He said, 'You're the man I'm looking for.'"

It took only three tries in the studio to lay down the horn track that became part of David Lee Roth's hit song.

"When you called, I got to thinking about what I'd done, what all I didn't do, and what all I wished I'd done," he said. "And I couldn't think of a thing I'd do different. I'm not saying I didn't have lots of ups and downs, but I wouldn't change a thing."

He still does play, and still blows lead in those familiar big band numbers.

"At my age, there is no way I can play as fast as I used to play, and I accept that fact," he said. "Today when I stand up and take a solo, I know the solo is not as good as it was in the good old days." He smiles and leans close. "But I know I'm going to do it better than anybody else!"

June 3, 2010

Blaggards

You think you have heard the Irish ditty *What Shall We Do with a Drunken Sailor?* Well, you have never heard it pounded out by a rock band thrashing electric guitar, thumping bass, pumping drums and screaming. Yes, there actually is an album credit for "violins and screaming."

Welcome to the new sound of world music, courtesy of a wave of Irish rockers such as Blaggards.

Good-bye to harps, fifes, and penny whistles. The fiddle endures, along with some salty lyrics, to create a whole new sound that is attracting kiddos who never would have been caught listening to Irish music.

The Irish rock movement began in Ireland in the 1970s, but seems to be more popular than ever.

Front man, guitarist and singer Patrick Devlin came over from Dublin while in his early 20's. He worked the Houston club scene, and noticed no one was filling the demand for Irish rock music. He started several versions himself, finally teaming up with bass player Chad Smalley in 2003 in a group that became Blaggards (there is no "the"–just "Blaggards").

They filled the Irish rock niche admirably. "Within weeks of forming, we found ourselves in high demand and were gigging constantly across Texas," Devlin said. They soon landed in Austin, where they added Chris Buckley to create their current setup. They tour and gig steadily. When I reached Devlin on the phone, he was in the middle of a 15-hour drive across the Midwest, where the band was returning from a pub tour.

It is fair to say that a Blaggards show may not be for the faint of heart. On their CD, they meld traditional folk and country songs with straight rock, turning familiar tunes into frenzied anthems. Imagine the lilting *Big Strong Man* in a medley with *Yakety Sax*. Or a frenetic version of Elvis's *Suspicious Minds*, punctuated with screaming fiddle? They even take *Folsom Prison Blues* and morph it into *The Fields of Athenry*.

"My mother listened to Elvis, Johnny Cash, and rockabilly," Devlin said. "My dad listened to traditional Irish music. I blame my A.D.D. for jumping around with the genre mixes. All of us in the band like to take left turns, and especially to do stuff people are not expecting."

Audiences may not expect it, but they like it. Blaggards fans range from their 20s to past 50. "When we do pub shows, the youngsters bring their parents for the early shows."

So, Blaggard Devlin, what can the audience expect? Should they be scared?

"They don't need to be warned, just be ready," he said. "We don't take kindly to people sitting down and politely clapping. They have to get up."

After hearing Blaggards, you will never listen *to Drunken Sailor* in quite the same way.

Trust me.

But you'll never forget it, either.

Hey ho and up she rises.

Sept 24, 2008

Will Owen-Gage: Scary Good

When I first heard Will Owen-Gage in 2005, he was so good it was scary. The guitar whiz was all of 17 years old. But be played his Stratocaster with the skill of 37 and the wisdom of 77.

Young guitar slingers come and go. Just as in basketball there is always the "next Michael Jordan," in music there is the "next Stevie Ray."

Owen-Gage doesn't want to be the next Stevie Ray; he wants to be the "first Will Owen-Gage."

"He was my number one influence," Owen-Gage admitted about the Vaughan comparison. "But it was more of a spiritual influence. I could feel his energy through his music."

Owen-Gage was also influenced by the music his dad and brothers listened to. Born in Kentucky, he was raised on bluegrass. In fact when I interviewed him, the consummate blues performer was backstage waiting to play at the Kentucky Music Weekend in Louisville. He also tuned in to the likes of the Grateful Dead and Jimi Hendrix. He absorbed it all and is well on his way to finding his own voice.

Describing music in words is like describing a painting in flavors. Suffice to say that Owen-Gage plays with confidence, creativity, and taste.

With many musicians, you detect patterns, riffs, cliched licks they use over and over. Give Owen-Gage five breaks in one blues song and he jumps on every one, playing something totally different each time. Every note is unexpected; yet every note is exactly right.

Just as he is always ready to step up for a lead, he knows how to back up and give someone else the stage–a trait rare even in more seasoned players.

Another attribute that sets him apart is that Owen-Gage is grounded in music theory. He attended a magnet school for musicians in San Antonio, so not only does he know the difference between phrygian and mixolydian scales, he knows when to use them.

"I am not focused on one sort of music," he told me during a gig at Waring's Steak Nite. "I am trying to become a musician instead of a bluesmeister."

But no one is thinking of scales when they see him on stage. In the middle of one Roots concert, it started to drizzle. Out came the sheets of plastic to cover the amps. After 40 minutes of waiting, Owen-Gage had had enough. He ripped off the plastic, plugged in his guitar, and said, "Let's play some music."

For the next hour his screaming guitar defied the gods of thunder and lightning and made the crowd forget the dangers of dancing next to a maniac playing electric guitar on a wet dance floor.

With his great guitar skill, Owen-Gage is not looking to sell out, whatever that means. He stays and plays the hill country in order to perfect his art.

"I'm not attracted to the Nashville scene," he said. "The Hill Country is bringing in good artists. The scene is genuine because musicians are not coming here to be discovered, but to become better musicians."

In Will Owen-Gage's case, that is a scary thought.

April 9, 2008

Dialogues and Dances

Mark Hierholzer wants to change the way you experience music. In the process, he might change the way you experience life.

This Saturday, Hierholzer–a graduate of the Eastman School of Music, published composer, director of the Fredericksburg Chorale, Mixed Choir and Arion Maennerchor, and "piano-playing son of a bitch"–presents the latest in his series of "Dialogues and Dances" at Zion Lutheran Church.

Hierholzer's innovative approach to composition began early in life, inspired by listening to 78-rpm records of Toscanini and Horowitz.

"My parents, while not particular fans of classical music, were very discriminate about things," Hierholzer recalled. "There was good music; there was bad. It was quite unforgiving."

Later he realized it was this discriminating attitude that led him to believe there are things in this world that are good; there are things that are bad; and "you strive to work toward the good things."

One of the good things he has sought to create is a more vibrant way of writing, performing, and relating to music.

"I think that there's been a tradition in choral music to create a certain choral 'sound,'" he said. "The interest is in the sound, and less on the communication of ideas. Modern culture has said there is no meaning in life. Once you have said there is no ultimate meaning to our existence in the universe, you cease to have anything to say musically. The only thing you can do then is make noise, and then you just sit around and talk about what kinds of noise you make. We never come from a choral recital and ask 'what was the choir communicating?'"

Communication is paramount in Hierholzer's creative process.

"Generally I write the words first," he said. "The tone, inflection, stop, and rise of the words becomes the foundation of the music. You try to keep the sound of the word as intact as possible. The challenge is that the music does have a powerful role in conveying the idea, but that it never overpowers the words."

Another challenge is convincing his singers to risk a new way of singing.

"The tone quality the modern choir makes is less than thrilling," Hierholzer said. "Human voices aren't the same; they don't naturally blend. You have to work at getting the guys to blend with the girls. Therefore the guys start to sing like girls and the girls have to do something to make themselves not sound like girls either. It removes us from our humanity."

Hierholzer exhorts his singers to allow their singing voices to sound as distinct as their speaking voices. The reception to this new way of vocalizing is mixed.

"I would say that it depends on the age group," he said. "Kids tend to respond much quicker; they don't ask questions. They see something that's lively and they like it. Adults, because they are in a set pattern, are more prone to be resistant. But many have said –and this is what I love to hear–'I initially hated this; now I find it really thrilling.'"

Audiences respond in much the same way.

"Many walk away saying 'this isn't what I came to hear,'" he admitted. "Then others say 'I've never heard anything like it.'"

"If you are doing something that is really valuable, you are going to have people walking away, there's no question about it. If you do that thing that makes everyone happy, half of them are going to be asleep in the process."

Therein lies the risk. But it is a risk Mark Hierholzer embraces.

"True beauty always has a component of danger as well as an element of benevolence in equal measure. About a year ago I was at the coast, sitting on the second story balcony. It was an amazing image at night of the ocean out there, just roaring. There was something so powerful about it even in calm weather that brings people to that place of awe.

"In the foreground there was a swimming pool. Now, a swimming pool is fun, but you wouldn't say the swimming pool was beautiful. There is just no comparison. One thing is beautiful beyond speech, and one aspect of that is the absolute danger of it.

"Great art, I believe, is always trying to grasp that truth that is built into the fabric of our universe. You can never really remove danger from beauty, and in short that is what these pieces are about."

Hierholzer's "Dialogues and Dances" are a way for the audience to share that risk.

"When you articulate ideas that you believe are good for yourself, you have to believe they are good for other people," he said. "I believe it can be good for people to let go of those things that are familiar and go to the place that for me, makes living 'living.' In this culture, it's easy to say 'I like this and you like this and that's fine.' I'm not willing to say that.

"If you allow yourself to get out of that routine, you'll find yourself open to listening. It's going to be thrilling."

Oct 19, 2005

Thomas Michael Riley:
Finally a Songwriter

Even after he had written 500 songs, including a Texas top ten hit, Thomas Michael Riley had a hard time convincing one person that he really was a songwriter: himself.

"Gary P. Nunn had picked up a couple of my songs, then a couple more, then he got up to about eight songs," Riley recalled. "I thought, wow, they must be pretty good because he put two of them on his *Greatest Hits Volume II*. But I still didn't believe in my heart that I was a songwriter."

Riley continued to work other jobs, including driving a moving van, working for a check printing company, even teaching high school. But finally there came a moment when he knew he had to follow his heart.

"You never know what your gifts are, until you finally know," he said. "It was when I wrote a song called *American Dream*... I thought, whoa... OK, Riley, you are a songwriter."

That is also when he realized he faced two choices: "fight it, or go with it." Thankfully for his growing number of fans, Riley decided to go for it.

Now the world can enjoy such songs as *Redneck Riviera* and *Cow Pasture Pool*, "the only song written about golf." That oblique approach makes Riley different from your average back porch picker.

He holds a degree in English ("I crammed four years of school into six and a half years"), and sprinkles quotes from Thoreau and

Emerson into his conversation. Fortunately, his stint teaching English did not hamper his songwriting ability.

"I was always going to write the Great American Novel, but I couldn't focus long enough," he said. "So then I went to short stories. I always enjoyed playing and singing, so that's when it hit me–it is songs. For me, that's the ultimate short story."

At first he had a hard time convincing the rest of the world to listen to his songs. Like many Texas musicians, he paid his dues playing dance halls and bars, where catching the nuances of a songwriter's brilliant wordplay was not a high priority for partying patrons. Riley learned to sneak up on his audience.

"I'd have to play three cover tunes then slip in an original," he said with a laugh. "You'd watch the dancers. If they didn't recognize a song, they didn't know how to dance to it, and your job was to keep them dancing. That is when I knew there was no future in playing other people's music."

Playing his own music paid off. Now the world is catching up.

"I like to see people dance–don't get me wrong," he explained. "I'm just proud now that they are dancing to my songs."

One challenge for singer songwriters is cultivating their own voice, different from all the other talented musicians. For Riley, the difference is basic.

"That's a tricky thing to do, to put your heart and soul into a song, and still have a rhythm that makes your audience feel what you are trying to convey," he said. "For me, it's not about any thing other than stuff I experienced; I just write from my perspective."

Another thing that sets him apart is his easy manner on stage.

"Songwriters are probably some of the worst performers," he noted. "A long time ago when I first started writing, I had the mindset that you all sit there and you listen to every word. Later I realized they are here for the same reasons I am–they want to enjoy life, they want to have a good time. If I can capture them with my songs, that's great."

Even with his recent success, Riley knows more opportunity lies ahead.

"I'm probably unknown in 99% of world," he said, laughing. "So I've got a little room to grow."

Aug 6, 2008

Stephanie Urbina Jones:
Back Where She Belongs

As she carved out her music career beyond the Texas Hill Country, Stephanie Urbina Jones always sought a larger stage. Today, the singer, songwriter–and now actress–is looking back at that Texas heritage to further her future success.

Not that she hasn't been enjoying a strong career. Jones was the first female Hispanic artist to go to #1 on the Texas Music chart, where she had #1 hits for five years in a row (with great titles such as *Como Se Llama, Mama* and *I'm Not a Pinata*). She played festivals across the state, and signed a record deal in Nashville on Clint Black's label.

Yet many residents of the Hill Country–where Jones was raised–are still unaware of the talented performer that grew up in their midst.

That is changing.

Jones's father was full-blooded Mexican-American; her mother, Anglo. When her mother remarried, the family moved to Fredericksburg. By the time Stephanie graduated from Fredericksburg High School, she had a path planned.

"I wanted to reconnect to that Hispanic heritage," she said. "There is so much joy, passion and love that comes from my Mexican-American heritage, I wanted to fuse my music with the culture and share it with the world."

Jones moved to Nashville where she was able to work with the legendary Texas Tornadoes. It was there she discovered what she calls her "gift of writing." She was working on staff at Sony Music, writing, recording demos. It was a fulfilling craft, but Jones wanted more. "I kept waiting for a Hispanic-American female to show up," she said. "Nobody did, so I thought maybe I should try."

It was natural for her to go from writing to performing, as evidenced by her early success. But as we all learned from music documentaries, the road to the top holds many dips. But a divorce and record label folding were not enough to slow Jones down.

"I am a very spiritual person," she said. "I love what I do, so I'm going to do it no matter what. This is not about being famous or rich. This is being able to communicate with music with the people you love."

Jones has had enough taste of the spotlight to know that is where she needs to be. "As you go up in this business, you get better sound systems, and better production values. I want to be able to afford to do that, yet be happy, creative, and continue to love what I am doing. I feel things are coming together again to take me to that point of really connecting with a huge audience."

Her road has taken her in some unexpected directions, such as playing female lead in a movie–*Courage*, a short western directed by William Booth. Even that fits in her plan. "I had the opportunity to see what it was like to work on a movie. The makeup, the clothes, the way so many elements come together to make it work–that is magic to me."

What does success look like to Stephanie Urbina Jones? "I am trying to get out of my own way about how it's supposed to look," she offered.

One of its faces was her pivotal project–the Texicana Concert Series.

Jones put together full-day celebrations of Hispanic heritage in Texas. She created the series in Luckenbach, and hosted them monthly in San Antonio, Austin, Corpus Christi, Boerne, and Luckenbach, with plans to add Dallas and Houston. The events included a concert performance, mariachis, jalapeno-eating contest, children's face painting, piñatas and more.

"I am passionate about my Texas and Hispanic roots. One of my greatest joys as a child was listening to the mariachis. I love singing with them, I love folkloric dance, I think it is beautiful."

Perhaps the most rewarding part of Jones's current path is the way her outward aura grows naturally from her inner being.

"So much of who I am is where I come from," she said. "Growing up in Fredericksburg, you never met a stranger. It is such a warm community. All of the cultures there, the importance of music, the independent spirit. You go to Luckenbach any day of the week, there is a picker's circle, with musicians carving out songs with their guitars. It was a great training ground."

And whenever she performs in the Hill Country, Stephanie Urbina Jones is right back where she belongs. "There is no place in the world I'd rather be than right there."

July 13, 2011

Champion fiddler Bart Trotter jamming with a young Sarah Jarosz

World Champion

Did you know that Fredericksburg is home to the 6-time National Champion Fiddle Player, the 1986 World Champion Fiddle Player, the 2-time First Runner-up at the Grand Masters Fiddle Contest, the 5-time Southwestern States Fiddle Champion, the 5-time winner of the New Mexico State Fair Fiddle Contest, and the 2-time winner of the U.S. Invitational Fiddle Contest?

Who are all these people?

Bart Trotter.

The musician who holds every single one of these honors moved from Ruidoso to Fredericksburg to be nearer to family, but Trotter–who grew up in Odessa–admits he missed Texas music.

That sweet swing sound was in his blood. His first memories of music were the fiddling of his great uncle, who played with Sons of the West and other bands in the 1930s and 40s. Young Trotter wanted to fiddle too, but the only route available to him was the school orchestra. So in sixth grade, his fingers began learning the violin. But his heart was pulled in another direction.

"I never really was much into classical music," he explained. "I loved going to fiddling contests on weekends."

Trotter led a double life. During the week he played violin in the school orchestra. On weekends, he escaped to fiddle contests where he began racking up awards. He stayed in orchestra throughout school, even as he played football for legendary Permian, partly because his friend fiddler Mark O'Conner encouraged him to take advantage of the free training.

These days, Trotter describes his fiddling style as Texas swing, tipping his baseball cap to music legends Benny Thomason and Major Lee Franklin for blazing that trail.

"It's kind of a mixture of bluegrass, swing, jazz, and blues," Trotter said, adding that his idol is Johnny Gimble, another legend in Texas music.

Trotter regularly plays with industry stars such as Gimble, including Gary P. Nunn, Merle Haggard, Cindy Cashdollar, Floyd Domino and a staggering list of musicians well known in the recording industry. Playing good music with great musicians is his passion.

"The best thing to me is getting to play with other musicians who are equal to or better than me," he said. "When you get a full stage of great musicians and start taking turns, it's really fun. Everybody inspires everyone else. That's when it's really magic."

Trotter stays involved in music off stage as well. He and his wife publish a series of tour guides for central Texas communities, and have started booking music talent for area clubs.

"We want to really promote live music in the hill country," he said. "We want to see even more live venues. It's great to walk in to a club and hear bluegrass, jazz, or country swing. We see Fredericksburg becoming a music destination."

With Bart Trotter living here, it already is.

May 17, 2006

Nate Mayfield:
From Baroque to Polka

Sitting in the back pew of Zion Lutheran church one Sunday, I heard a glorious sound from above.

It was the pure, powerful tone of a trumpet.

Just to make sure Gabriel was not making a premature appearance, I climbed the balcony. For the remainder of the service, I enjoyed a back row seat to a remarkable performance on piccolo trumpet by Nathaniel Mayfield accompanied on organ by Mark Hierholzer.

It was not the place for an interview. But I was able to corner Mayfield later at a no less sacred venue–Oktoberfest. Somehow the

Julliard graduate and "one of the most talented baroque trumpeters in the world" had gotten roped into performing with the Polkamatics, which is like cellist Yo Yo Ma playing with the Yo Mamas.

But maybe not. The first thing he wanted to talk about was how the delicate baroque trumpet was related to the alphorn, that long curved instrument used by Swiss farmers to call in their cows. Those opposing qualities are what drew Mayfield to the trumpet.

"My mother is a brilliant musician with a beautiful voice," he said. "I took my musicality from her, and from my father I took his rugged Texas strength. The trumpet has been a perfect fusion of those extremes."

The young man tried other instruments, but none spoke to him with the trumpet's voice. His battle with the trumpet is to play it as musically as possible, while honoring its power. "No other instrument gives me that type of sound quality and difficulty of merging musicality and strength. I am always trying to superimpose those two sides of my life."

So how does one of the world's foremost performers on baroque trumpet–an incredibly difficult instrument to master–rationalize playing *Mein Hut er hat drei Ecken* at a street festival?

He set down his beer.

"Each represents different parts of humanity. This," he said, gesturing at the revelers, "to me represents happiness and letting go. It is easily understood and approachable, and just fun. Playing baroque music is more serious. It explores man's relationship with God through the art of classical music."

Is one approach more vital?

"It is hard to say," he said. "I think this is in some sense even more vital. It is important for people to be happy and to enjoy their lives. Of course there is the responsibility we have to always push ourselves, to find the highest ideal."

Mayfield has pursued his higher ideals, with studies at The Juilliard School, Columbia University, Interlochen Arts Academy, Tanglewood Institute, and the Hochschule für Musik in Karlsruhe, Germany. It shaped his belief that studying and performing the highest level of music ever written is a way to touch people's souls.

"I love hymns, four part harmony, descants," he said. "I feel they are a real celebration of man's ability–through reason–to have a relationship with God. You know, there is a saying that not every musician believes in God, but they all believe in Bach. I think there is some truth to that just because of what it sparks in our basic core of humanity. Reason is as much a component of faith as the emotional side."

Over time, Mayfield will take his message and his music to Switzerland, Canada, New York, and Hawaii.

"I enjoy jetting around and playing baroque trumpet. But today," he said, picking up his beer and heading for his seat in the front row of the horn section, "it is Oktoberfest and polkas. Why not?"

Oct 29, 2008

Fiddling Sisters

Every few years, the music business seems to discover its "next big stars." Just as often, the glow quickly fades. But the Quebe Sisters Band might be the group to make those stars align again.

These young ladies are what popular music can always use: fresh, eager, enthusiastic artists passionately in love with what they do, and thoroughly trained to do it well. As a bonus they are bright, polite, grounded, and well spoken.

The Quebe Sisters Band consists of Grace (22), Sophia (20), and Hulda Quebe (17), homeschooled sisters from north Texas who just started playing in 1999. The girls came from a family that had no musical performing experience at all. Ten years ago they happened to hear someone fiddling at a fiddle contest, and "just fell in love" with the sound.

Sherry McKenzie was their first fiddle instructor. Right from the start, Sherry saw that all three sisters demonstrated astonishing talent and determination and a real love of music. Soon her husband, Joey, three-time world champion fiddler, joined in the teaching and arranging. He now plays rhythm guitar for the band, with Drew Phelps on upright bass.

They are booked at fairs, festivals, corporate events and shows across America, and came to Fredericksburg to play at the Pioneer Museum's Roots Music concert. I spoke with Hulda, who was only 7 when she first caught fiddle fever.

"Ever since that time we have just loved to play and had a great time doing it," she said. They love it so much that they practice six days a week. "It pays off. You always have more fun out jamming if you have done your homework. "

Musically, the band has struck a successful balance of staying true to the western swing tradition while adding its own fresh touches. One reviewer described it as, "Bob Wills meets the Andrews Sisters."

"We try to do a version of an old song that is true to the style–we don't like all new versions," Hulda said. "People say it sounds like stuff back in that era, but we like to add our own variations of different parts. Working out songs that way is one of unique things about this band. It is fun to do."

Their act is also inspirational to fans of all generations.

"Our style of music and what we do is really just try to be whole-some," Hulda said. "We want to be a real Christian influence. People come up say they like your music, the way you dress, and what you play–it is good, timeless music, and it never gets old. The people who played it were great musicians, and it will be played for generations. A lot people are attracted to that."

The band continues to build its following through CD sales and Internet videos. But they hold no illusions of breaking out into the mainstream music world.

"There are not tons of kids who are into this kind of music, so we are not really mainstream," Hulda conceded. Fame is not high on the list of priorities. They have already garnered interest from different music labels, but they "want to be careful" as they lay out their careers.

"We are not playing every single night, or playing music we don't want to play," she said. "We want to be successful, but still have fun. The main thing is to stay true to our values and to what we believe in."

Hulda had another message for the community.

"Tell them," she said, "that if they are fans of western swing they should come out. We play classic western music. Even if you have not heard of it, it is a great fun style, in a family atmosphere."

"And," she added, "we put on a pretty good show."

Aug 13, 2008

John Arthur Martinez:
Second on Nashville Star;
First in Hearts

As a top finisher on the first season of *Nashville Star*, John Arthur Martinez impressed millions of viewers. But what makes him most proud is the effect he had on one fan.

Not long ago the country singer-songwriter received a note from a young man who wanted to tell him that Martinez had saved his life.

"He said he heard me 20 years ago at a bar in Tucson, singing a song called *22*–a simple song about the possibilities a 22-year-old has in front of him," Martinez said. "That night he asked for a recording. I told him I hadn't recorded it, so he had me write down the lyrics on a cocktail napkin. Two decades later, he told me he had contemplated suicide before coming to the club that night. Every time after that when he had dark thoughts, he took out that cocktail napkin."

The fan had no idea Martinez had been on television. In the first year of the country talent show *Nashville Star*, Martinez finished second. That exposure led to a new connection with legions of fans, a record deal, and lots of interest in his career.

I asked the Austin native about the culture of "music as competition" that shows such as *American Idol* and *Nashville Star* promote.

"On a personal note, music should not be a competition," Martinez said. "That is not necessarily the way music was intended to be discovered. But this is a free enterprise system, and Americans love to decide who is the 'champion.' That is part of who we are."

He also recognizes the fact that music is very much a business. And Martinez is very much the entrepreneur–one of those rare musicians who has figured out how to make a living doing what he loves. He tours, records, sells CDs, and has a robust web presence.

And he has the ability to write songs, which he attributes to his double major in English and Broadcast Journalism.

"Journalism teaches you to be very concise," he explained. "If you haven't captured your audience in the first few sentences, you've lost them. It is the same with songwriting. If people are not excited about what you are singing in the first few seconds, they are going punch that button."

It is Martinez who is punching his fans' buttons.

"There are folks like the father of an autistic child, whose son watched me on *Nashville Star*," he said. "I sang a ridiculous song with all kinds of poetic devices–alliteration, assonance, tongue-twisters. His son tried to sing along–it was the first time he ever uttered any words at all. His dad bought my CD, and his child eventually started playing piano."

Stories like that tell Martinez that whatever he is doing is worth doing–even if it affects only a few individuals.

"I don't want to be just about creating a product that steers people to the bar," said the man who knows a bit about being a TV product. "If my lyrics touch people, then I feel like I have been a successful singer-songwriter."

Oct 1, 2008

Fresh and New, Times Two

The Rankin Twins are just so... so... well, so darn adorable. But don't let that fool you. They are tough, smart, funny, and talented musicians who know what they are doing on stage and off.

"It doesn't matter what people think," said Amy and April Rankin, the singing identical twins, of their bubbly personalities. "We know who we are. Sure we can get really excited. We can't help our personalities. But we both have degrees."

Their natures are contagious, gregarious, delicious. Whether they are onstage singing, on the radio talking about their music, or posting on Facebook ("love yer guts"), they revel in their fans.

"Both of us are huge 'people persons.' We love meeting people, and want to have as many friends as possible." Amy took a job at Starbucks just so she could be surrounded by people she hadn't met yet.

This joy in life is balanced by a pragmatic side. Not only do they both hold degrees from Texas A&M (Amy in Marketing; April in Ag Development), they have worked in corporate America, and they run a successful business–Twinty Photography.

With all their savvy, they were probably the last to know they were going to be in the music business. The twins had always shared a big love for music, but were more into athletics than singing.

"Our mom was shy, so she put us on stage for everything. We would sing, but not professionally." On Christmas Eve, they would perform for their family and neighbors, lip syncing to Madonna or the Judds. It wasn't until they were in junior high that they "realized we could actually sing."

They remember the first time they thought music might be a viable career choice. It was at a Barbara Mandrell concert.

"We were looking at the musicians on stage and suddenly had the gut feeling that we wanted to be up there doing that!"

In addition to their talent, they have an undefeatable sense of humor. They laugh at everything life throws at them. The biggest laugh was for the darkest moment.

After graduation, Amy underwent two surgeries to remove a brain tumor. How did they react? First, Amy coped with it by writing *Headaches & Heartbreaks*. Next, they made fun of it.

"We named the tumor 'Wally' because he was the size of a walnut," they laughed. After that scare, doctors discovered she had a cyst. So they named it "Cid."

"I joked that someday I would write a kids book called *The Adventures of Wally and Cid* because of my attitude," Amy said. "It would have a positive outlook, showing that if you think good things will happen, they will."

The Portland, Texas, natives have built their personal and professional lives around this philosophy.

"We think that on a weekly basis, something good will happen to us." It may be as simple as going to the mailbox. "We love getting mail. We say, oh my gosh, we got a FedEx package! This week we booked a show for November. That is our exciting thing for this week."

Make no mistake: the Rankins are serious about their music. They are patient and focused in building their band and their brand.

"We know we probably could make more money as a cover band, but that is not ultimately what we want to do. That's what has taken us so long. We know we can sing, but this scene is all about original music. We didn't put a band together until we had written some original songs."

So where are the Rankins headed?

"To the top," they said together. "We want to be everywhere. We want to be touring all over the U.S., then in Europe, just to put our music out there for everyone to hear." One of their goals this year is to book tour dates outside of the Lone Star State. "While we are fresh and new, why not be that way for other states, too?"

Whether taking pictures, talking on the radio, or performing on stage, the twins always are having fun.

"We love how you call our interaction with fans 'delicious' because that's how we feel about it too. Besides, that's just our personalities!"

Aug 10, 2011

CC McCartney: That "God" Voice

You have heard his voice. But you would not recognize him if he sat beside you.

I have, and I didn't.

C.C. McCartney was an unobtrusive presence that evening at Hondo's, wearing sunglasses and hat pulled low on his forehead. You wouldn't notice him until he opened his mouth. Then you couldn't ignore him.

"They call us 'the God voice,' the voice that brags about the radio station," he explained in response to my question asking what voice imaging was. He lowered his chin to his chest, took a breath and demonstrated. "Nobody plays more legends than we do... period... KKYX. That sort of thing."

The rolling, golden sound of McCartney and his ilk is the glue that holds radio shows together, or, as he explained, "I am the comma in the paragraphs of television and radio. Those are called voice images. It is sort of hard to explain what I do. But when you hear someone say 'WLS Chicago,' or 'Straight from the heart... FOX news,' that is what I do."

McCartney got his start while in college at a little radio station in Beeville, and admits he knew absolutely nothing. But when his friend, Barry Kaye (also a radio legend) asked him to come down for a summer, McCartney was immediately enraptured.

"I saw all that equipment and thought, wow, this is like Star Trek," he recalled. It didn't intimidate him when the station owner said, "You have one week to sound like a disk jockey or you are out of here."

"Some 42 years later I guess I must have passed that test," he said.

McCartney is now based in Nashville. He services radio and TV clients around the world, painting pictures with his voice. With digital recording and the Internet, he can deliver mp3 files to stations across the U.S., Canada, and overseas. For seven years he hosted a syndicated radio show in Tokyo without setting foot in Japan. When he finally flew over, he "was mobbed" and even made a guest appearance on their top comedy show.

Though he has worked many times on television, McCartney is most at home in a soundproof booth huddled behind a microphone.

"I just like radio a whole lot better, because I can envision the reaction in the theater of the mind," he said. "When I say it, I mean it. I don't read scripts verbatim. I get their intent, then I emote; then I act."

His attention to detail is legendary. He has been known to fly into a town and just listen to the radio for two days before he records.

"I will know how the jocks sound, the tempo, and the feel of the station," he explained. "When I get home, I am already part of the mix."

His sincerity and passion have garnered him top ratings in major cities, bucketsful of industry awards, and now induction as the newest member of the Texas Radio Hall of Fame.

"I am one of the top five disk jockeys in the history of rock and roll radio," he said. "When you hear my voice, you'll know who it is because it's a unique voice. That is not braggadocio. I have a passion for it. Tomorrow I will be better than I was today. And I had better be a whole lot better next Monday, or I'm not going to be a happy man."

Want to hear for yourself? McCartney is as close as your car radio.

"If you get in your car, tune in to 680 AM," he said. "You can hear me in San Antonio. I listened to myself all the way down here."

Aug 26, 2008

Classic Autumn

As a very young child, Autumn Boukadakis begged her parents to let her take piano lessons. Unlike most of us who never made it past Suzuki I, Autumn stuck with her lessons and received her degree in Classical Piano from the University of Texas. But rather than playing Brahms and Beethoven, Autumn was more influenced by the Dylan and Creedence tunes her dad played as she was growing up.

I discovered Autumn last fall while she was performing at the Auslander. With no preconception of what to expect, I was instantly drawn to her original style of singing and playing. She classifies it as folk/Americana, incorporating bits of gospel, rock, and country ballad.

The first thing I wanted to know was whether her classical training was a help or hindrance. It may seem a question with an obvious answer, but I've often envied the spirited performances of musicians uninhibited by music theory and formal training.

74

Her answer? Both.

"Classical training enabled me to really play technically challenging material, and I consistently try to apply that training in my own songwriting," she said. "But I have found that it may have hindered my improvisation skills. I am much more comfortable reading music, but improvising on stage is thrilling. It is just two completely different ways of playing music, and sometimes I lean on one more than the other."

It has not hindered her songwriting ability, as Autumn has released her second CD–*Velvet Sky*, a professionally-done work which has been described as a love letter to life.

"I was as truthful as I could possibly be," she explained. "A lot of reflection, a lot of sincerity, and plenty of musicality. The new album is more mature, classic, and a giant leap into a more focused folk/ Americana category."

Back to that "category" thing. Reviewers are always trying to pigeonhole a performer's sound, while performers squirm just as hard to avoid labels.

"I don't really compare myself to other artists, I just don't," she said. "Otherwise I would go crazy trying to live up to some vision of what is normal or right. Besides, calling myself folk/Americana 'with lots of room' sounds like a Starbucks order."

Fans can figure that all out for themselves, as Autumn returns to The Auslander this Friday for a rare Fredericksburg appearance. Those performances may become less rare, as the Oklahoma native is growing to love this Texas town.

"Out of all the cities in this fine country, Fredericksburg has been the most supportive," she noted. "I love the Auslander, I love KFAN, I love the hot tub at the Fredericksburg Inn. I sincerely love Fredericksburg; I intend to live there someday. The people are kind and they appreciate songwriters. Fredericksburg feels like family to me."

Autumn already has a friendly suggestion for her new Fredericksburg family.

"Get off the couch and come watch some live music," she said. "There is nothing that compares to sitting in a Biergarten, drinking Chimay, watching a live performance. Plus, Ray Rodriguez (Mystiquero) will be sitting in with us. And he is hot!"

Classic.

Feb 11, 2009

Jim Cullum Spices up Church

Fredericksburg boasts so much good live music, even the churches bring in nationally-recognized entertainment.

Aficionados of fine music and delicious food will enjoy both when American jazz icon Jim Cullum stops by to add spice to the St. Barnabas Jazz Fest.

His namesake Jim Cullum Jazz Band swings out at The Landing on the San Antonio Riverwalk, and is heard on more than 150 public radio stations on *Riverwalk, Live From The Landing*.

"This guy has played at Carnegie Hall, at the Kennedy Center, and hosts a National Public Radio show," event co-chair Stan Shannon said. "It is an honor having a world-class musician in Fredericksburg."

Bringing swing to churches is nothing new for Cullum, who is known for performing jazz masses around the area, including one in Fredericksburg.

"When Jim played here three years ago we had 450 people," Shannon said. "It was the biggest turnout for mass in the history of our church!"

For this Fredericksburg appearance, Cullum put together what he calls a "collective improvised ensemble." The group includes Cullum on cornet, clarinetist Ron Hockett, plus a keyboard and perhaps another rhythm player.

"It's really more of a chamber ensemble," Cullum told me during a phone interview. "We'll be playing mostly jazz standards."

Cullum is very clear on what the audience won't hear.

"We categorically avoid what we call the 'Top 18'–those abused Dixieland tunes such as *When the Saints Go Marching In*," Cullum said. "There is nothing wrong with those particular tunes, but they are played the same way just about everywhere. I try to swing and play the best ideas I can think of, while trying to get the best sound I can come up with."

Getting that sound is a constant quest for Cullum and his players.

"The same instrument can be sometimes dark and soft, and sometimes bright and brassy. That's the challenge," he said. "That's what I'm about. That's what I do every time I pick up the horn. I try to make the music as interesting and beautiful as I can."

Cullum admits having disdain for players who dazzle for the sake of dazzling. It points out the paradox great musicians face.

"We work hard to develop technique all our lives," he said. "Then the goal is to make the technique invisible. We never want the technique to get in the way of an idea. It doesn't matter if you can play higher or faster; it's wasting your music. You only have a limited number of arrows in your quivers so there is no sense in wasting them."

Shannon noted that the event's fundraising focus shifted after Hurricane Katrina struck the Gulf coast.

"Originally we were going to raise money to help with repairs in the local church," Shannon said. "But when they discovered 18 churches were destroyed in New Orleans, we changed the focus. We may have a leaky roof, but we can put a bucket under it."

"And it was fine with Jim," Shannon added, "since he has so many friends in New Orleans."

"We have done a lot of things for churches over the years," said Cullum, who can accommodate very few of the hundreds of benefit requests he receives. "I feel it's something I can do."

Oct 5, 2005

High Valley

You really should make an effort to go hear the band High Valley at the Rockbox Theater. After all, they traveled 2,852 miles to get here.

When I called Brad Rempel, oldest of three brothers in this up and coming family band, he was loading the van for their 8-hour trip from La Crete, Alberta, Canada to the nearest airport. (He casually reported it was 22 degrees F below zero–air temperature, not windchill.)

The band was heading to Nashville for the first stop on their current road trip. The 8-hour drive to the airport does not intimidate our hardy northern neighbors, even including literally having to drive across a frozen river.

"It beats driving to Nashville," he explained. "That is a 45-hour trip. But we have done it quite a few times."

Regular trips across North and Central America have been the key to High Valley's success at such an early age. Though all three brothers–Brad, Curtis, and Bryan–are younger than 25, they have been playing as a band for 13 years, and singing together their entire lives. In a town like La Crete, everyone sings.

"We grew up singing together as a family," Rempel said. "In the Mennonite church, harmony is part of the worship service. Everyone in town knows how to sing harmony."

The boys' religious and rural upbringing are at the heart of the band's music and mission. Their grandfather was shunned from a Mennonite colony in Mexico for committing the cardinal sin of buying a truck. The rest of the community still used buggies.

"He kind of thought outside the box," Rempel said.

Nonplussed, he relocated his family to La Crete, another Mennonite community perched on the upper reaches of Alberta, roughly parallel with Juneau. Farming is the major local industry, and the Rempel boys spent many hours riding tractors across fields of canola and wheat. One of their original songs is called *On The Combine*.

"I wrote lot of songs on that combine," Rempel said. "That's definitely in our favor when we perform it live. Everybody has story about growing up or spending time on farm. And people in the city are intrigued about us living out in the sticks."

That rural upbringing also keeps them grounded. Even performing live on the Canadian Country Music Awards for 1 million viewers, sharing the stage with Reba McEntire and Martina McBride, didn't get them out of doing their chores.

"When we get home, Dad still puts us to work digging out a grain bin or working on a tractor," Rempel said, laughing.

While they cherish their roots, they also recognize their good fortune.

"Music is totally an escape for us. Everybody in La Crete grows up working at a sawmill or on a farm. It's not that we hated the idea of staying in town, but we always dreamed of getting outside the box. We have been blessed with incredible experiences."

In their travels, they make it a point to visit as places like their hometown as they can.

"We play every single small town we can possibly find. Every town has its story. Small towns have been our bread and butter the last 10 years."

Because of that work ethic–performing 110 concerts in 5 months–and their fresh sound, High Valley landed a record deal, management and booking agent. Their music reflects their background: it's country but not corny, bluegrass but not boring. All their live shows feature mandolin, acoustic guitar, bass, and drums.

"If you can imagine Diamond Rio or Alabama starting up in 2010, that is our sound. It's country, but more organic, more acoustic, and of course more harmony."

The band mostly likes to sing of positive things, family, hard work, and faith.

"We set out making music–not to pay the bills, but to make music. Our music appeals to all ages, and it's great for the whole family. We tell the stories behind the songs. Everybody is going to leave encouraged and hopefully laughing as well. That's something all of America could use right now."

Jan 6, 2010

Playing from the Hill Country

People who reflect the character of the Texas Hill Country

Gregg Cheser

Characters

One day I was thinking about Gregg Cheser.

It's OK if you don't know him. Because you know someone like Gregg Cheser.

I was thinking about Gregg because I was sitting in a memorial service on Friday for another Fredericksburg resident. It made me remember the time I spoke at Gregg's memorial service in that same funeral home 10 years ago.

Gregg was a singer and songwriter who played in bands that opened for Jimi Hendrix and Janis Joplin. He was a man of quick wit, great compassion, and kind soul, and someone who challenged me musically and mentally.

Most of all, he was a colorful character. After moving to Texas from Kentucky, he became a fixture at the emerging Luckenbach scene, and performed solo and with his band The Pronto Brothers.

In between gigs he delivered Lone Star beer around town, following the philosophy of Cheatham Street Warehouse proprietor Kent Finlay, who used to say, "We sell all the beer we can't drink."

We lost Gregg in 2004, way too early. When it happened, I received a call from his family. They were arranging a funeral, and asked if I would say a few words at the service. If you have never been asked to do such a thing, let me tell you it is an incredible honor and incredibly frightening. I accepted, then spent several days walking around composing–and rejecting–many ideas. You see, it is almost impossible to say something at momentous events–whether weddings, graduations, or funerals–that hasn't been said and said and said. Those who know me know that I place a premium on being original: cliches are my enemy, and funerals are crawling with cliches.

Then it struck me. "Being original" exactly described Gregg Cheser. He was a good musician, a good father, a good man. But most of all, Gregg Cheser was a character.

A "character" is someone who is one of a kind. And Gregg was like no other kind. He had eccentricities, he vexed me, he kept me off balance, he frustrated me, he inspired me. But he engaged me! He never took the conventional path. I grew to love his "unexpectedness," and missed it greatly when he left us.

So that is what I spoke about at his service. Looking back, that small homily really set the template for the writing of these columns that began in 2005.

When it comes to deciding what to write about, I'm not trying to describe the best or most worthy musicians, or review their body of work. I'm not sanctioning one group over another. I have always looked most to those musical "characters," who use the art to stamp their personality and vision on the world. It might be the singer/songwriter, but it has also been the opera singer, the dulcimer player, the grandfather who recorded his first CD, the grandmother who learned to play cello, or the schoolteacher who plays kitchen utensils. They are all "characters."

What would our world be like if we all acted like our parents told us we were expected to act? What if everyone was just like you? Lord, what a dreary, uninteresting place. I wouldn't want to live in a world full of me's.

So, embrace those characters you are lucky enough to have stumble into your life. Embrace those who are different, challenging, or interesting.

Sure, they might make you uncomfortable.

But "comfortable" is not always the best place to be.

Aug 7, 2013

Russ Cox: Another Good Story

"This is a good story...."

A chat with Russ Cox is a tumble into a wonderland of stories and tales of a career laced with characters larger than life–starting with himself.

"Have a seat, by golly," he said, his face etched in a perpetual grin framed by burnished cheeks. "Ask me everything."

So I asked how Russ Cox would describe Russ Cox–a cowboy poet, singer of western songs, character actor?

"I don't know," he replied, "I'm always leery of saying I'm an artist, but that is probably what I ought to do. I'm better at painting than anything."

The Texas native ("fifth generation on my mom's side; third on my dad's") grew up in Houston, where he aspired to be an artist in the vein of Charlie Russell. Cox described Russell as one of his heroes, because "he was a cowboy first, and a painter after."

Cox is a cowboy, first, last, and always. He came to the Hill Country in '68. You could easily assume it was 1868, watching him strum his guitar, wearing high boots, cotton breeches, vest, collarless shirt, and wide-brimmed cowboy hat. The circumstances around Cox leaving Houston hinted at another story–something about escaping the love of an oilman's daughter.

"She was older, but I fell smooth in love with her," he said. "I didn't want to leave, but I had to..." He trailed off, then launched into a tale about his first job with another legend: Hondo Crouch.

"Hondo was 'notoriously thrifty,'" Cox remembered. "He'd send me to Stein Lumber, so I could buy #3 grade lumber that was warped and full of knots. I put one of those biggest boards on the top of a gate, and using a horseshoe rasp, a screwdriver, and a hammer, I chiseled an Alamo-style top on the wide board. When Hondo came back on Sunday to see how it was going, we went down to the back pasture where the new gate was. He pulls up, with a big old plug of tobacco in his mouth, and says, 'Looks like the horses chewed it.' Arghhh... he got me!"

Cox laughed.

He is not sure what caused his affinity for the old west. It goes as far back as he can remember.

"I always had it," he said. "There are pictures of me in elementary school that show I dress now like I did then. I had to have my ma make up some of those bib front shirts."

Cox's avocation has brought him to the attention of Hollywood producers who come looking for authentic western props and characters. Cox has supplied wagons, hats, clothes, and equipment to several production companies, appeared as an extra, and had speaking parts in four or five movies. He was a featured player in *The Wind and the Lion*, with Sean Connery and Candice Bergan ("I played the Marine sergeant who gets winged in the arm").

These days Cox "builds fires, and cuts taters and onions" in between singing at events with Bill Walding, who sets up a chuckwagon for private parties and public events.

"I usually stick with old, old cowboy songs," he explained. "When I learn a new song it might be new to me but it might have been written in 1908."

He grins, and starts singing one he wrote called *Hondo's Hat*.

We're not sure why she did it
We don't know where it's at
We only know one night at the dance
Some gal took Hondo's hat...
...If she'd a known what it meant to him
She'd a left that battered hat
Cause his hat was his friend
Through many a mile
Through many a song and beer
Now the one so precious to him
Is just someone's souvenir
If only she'd return it
I'd get her one that fit
After all what good is Hondo's hat
Without Hondo under it?*

The crowd claps. Cox grins.
"Here's another good story..."
Nov 21, 2007

*Hondo's Hat, words and music by Russ Cox, used by permission

The Boogie Man

Deejay Barry Kaye wants to meet every single KHLB listener. He already knows most of them by their first name.

"Hey, our friend Phil is driving to Kerrville right now," I heard him say one morning as I listened to 102.5 FM. "Phil, here's a song for you... turn up your radio!"

I had to smile. He remembered a comment I had made during our interview, and used it to personalize his show the next morning. I heard him do it over and over as he dropped the names of listeners within hearing distance of the 50,000-watt radio station perched just off the square in tiny Mason, Texas.

How did this radio legend–who has had a 40-year career as "The Boogie Man," invented Top 40 FM radio, recorded top country hits, performed at the Country Music Association's Fan Fare, worked with every major act of the 60s, 70s, and 80s, owned the second-largest dance hall in the world, was top on-air personality in Houston, Dallas, Los Angeles, and is in the Texas Radio Hall of Fame–wind up doing the morning show in Mason?

While he grew up in Corpus Christi, it turns out that Kaye had been coming to the Mason area since he was 11 years old. His best buddy's family would come here to visit, and he often tagged along. His radio career took him away, but about 10 years ago he was able to find the ranch of his dreams. He retired ("sort of"), hoping to do a little Internet radio work and hunt on his own property.

When his radio production business didn't quite live up to expectations, Kaye was faced with going back to work on the deejay circuit. That was a problem.

"I didn't want to leave my ranch," he confessed. So he started to contact local radio stations about going back on the air. That was another problem. "They didn't believe me!" While everyone had heard of him, no one thought he was serious about working in smaller markets. Kaye was serious. One radio station manager told him that it paid little, and he'd have to scrub toilets. "I said, I'll take a little and I scrub a mean toilet. But they never called me back."

So the irrepressible Kaye applied at the local Super S and got a job in their gas station.

"I worked a year at $7.25 an hour," he said. "I became a 'groceryologist.' I could get you gas, chips ,and dip so fast you wouldn't believe it." He took pride in his job. "My buddies from radio would come to town and I'd be in my little Super S outfit, cleaning out the squeegee buckets. I heard them make excuses for me. I said you don't have to apologize–I love this job! It didn't bother me a bit."

That job at the Gas Hut may have been the best training for his KHLB gig.

"I see that was a blessing, now, because I got to meet everyone. There is not a human being I don't know, because everyone came to get gas and food."

Kaye is capitalizing on those connections with his "Barry Kaye Tour."

"I thought there were two things when I first came to work that I had to do as fast as possible. I knew I had to come up with a way to mention names on radio, and I had to bring attention to the station that we are live and local."

His solution was to get out on the street, Literally. He started driving his Kia Rio "limo" ("it's about 4 feet long") to visit every town– Harper, Doss, Junction, Brady, Hext, Yates, Pontotoc, Skeeterville, Melvin, Calf Creek.

"I feel I can't talk about these people unless I've stood there, even if there is only one store and a house."

He has walked into every store and shaken hands, telling everyone he meets exactly at what time he is going to say "hi" to them on the air.

"If you tell them you are going to mention them, they'll listen. If they tell 10 people who tell 10 other people, in a small town it won't take a week for everyone to know."

It hasn't all been easy. But Barry Kaye is the kind of guy who turns lemons into lemon meringue pie. He tells the story of a listener who called into the show the first week and said, "I've been listening to you for four days now, and you are really starting to irritate me."

Instead of being offended, Kaye gave him a daily segment where he calls in to complain about something.

Kaye even started the Hometown Country Club, with the goal of having a correspondent in each of the towns.

"Once you win them over, they realize you are a real person," he said. "You have got to become one of their family members. You have to be genuine and down-home good folk in the Texas Hill Country or you are not going to last."

And "lasting" is one thing he wants to be.

"This is my last hurrah. I didn't think I'd ever have another shot at being good on radio. I haven't been this excited in years. They are letting me be me, going on the air and having fun again. Radio is fun here, buddy!"

March 23, 2011

Pat Friday

She is where movie star Lynn Bari found her voice and how Joe Friday got his name.

She is Fredericksburg resident Pat Friday, a delightful wisp of a woman who at the age of 15 hobnobbed with stars of film, stage and radio.

As Helen Patricia Freiday, she first found fame by winning a college singing contest. The prize was a guest appearance on a national radio show–Bing Crosby's *Kraft Music Hall*. She made quite the impression.

"The mail from my appearance was so heavy, they bought me–quite literally," she said.

As Pat Friday (she dropped the "e" from her last name), she became a regular on the show, guested on all the popular radio programs of the era, and even hosted the *Kraft Music Hall* over two summers.

The young Friday spent her days in college, rehearsed in the evenings, and broadcast the show once a week. In her radio appearances, Friday worked with all the big names of her day. Here is a lightning round of her impressions of these larger-than-life personalities:

George Burns:

"He was a wonderful person. When Franklin Roosevelt died, Mr. Burns called me and said it wouldn't be appropriate to do a funny show that day. I said I'll sing. He said, get here fast. I was on his radio show many times."

Gracie Allen:

"Her character was not the person she was. You have to be bright to act that dumb. Her puns were wonderful."

Jack Benny:

"What a nice man."

Victor Borge:

Friday was the featured singer on his show every week. "He was one of the finest people I've ever known. His wife was even finer. They were so happy together they made you feel warm. He was a good father, a very good friend, and a fabulous musician."

Bob Hope:

Friday remembers working with him on the Armed Forces Radio Service that were broadcast all over the world. "I was blessed by meeting wonderful people, wonderful talent."

Benny Goodman:

Friday worked with Goodman on Armed Forces Radio. One evening she went to dinner and the famed clarinetist recognized her from the bandstand. "He sent someone over to ask if I would get up to sing," she said. "I replied, 'I have been dreaming of it.'"

Glenn Miller:

The great bandleader was working on a film that featured the actress Lynn Bari. As was common practice in those days, studios would bring in ghost singers to voice the songs of the movie stars. Miller signed Friday to do both *Sun Valley Serenade* in 1941 and *Orchestra Wives* the following year. She earned $500 per film, made no residuals or royalties, received no credit, and was even forbade from telling anyone she was the singer.

That was the way the Hollywood machine ground in those days. I asked her impressions of one more radio star–Bing Crosby. Reluctantly she told the tale of working with the Crosbys. They were not happy at her decision to marry, since it would finish her as "The Singing Coed." The powerful family went so far as to blackball her in Hollywood, a sentence later lifted by their mother.

And finally, Jack Webb:

Pat Friday did a radio show with him called *In Time To Come*. It lasted only 13 weeks, but Jack Webb was destined to go on to greater things.

"He asked me one day, how long are you going to be using your name?" Friday said. "He told me he may adopt it, and I said that's OK."

As fans of the radio and TV series *Dragnet* know, Webb became Sergeant Joe Friday.

Interestingly, her fondest memories are not about her brushes with celebrities. She prefers to remember the times she spent volunteering, helping out homeless, soldiers, folks down on their luck.

"On those shows where you were 'paid' money to perform, well, some were fun, some were not," she said. "Some were a hoot, some were.... hoochie. The best part was the volunteer work I did during the war, for the USO, Command Performance, and Armed Forces Radio Service."

Friday is active in the community, still volunteering. Her one frustration is that she cannot remember all the details of those heady days.

"At my age they say you should remember the past with total clarity," she said. "Balderdash! I can't, without the bits and pieces to support it."

She laments the loss all those photos, scrapbooks, and especially her sheet music. Sheet music?

"How would you feel if you had a piece of sheet music that had inscribed on it from Ira Gershwin: 'Finally! Someone sang Summertime as a lullaby. Thank you. Thank you!' I grieve that I lost that."

As we celebrate that we found Pat Friday.

July 14, 2010

Two Views

Let's go!

If you have lived in Fredericksburg for any length of time since 1993, chances are good you have met Tani Guthrie and Dran Hamilton. Maybe in the aisles of the grocery store. Or volunteering at the Pioneer Museum's Fassel House ("Be sure you tell them to pronounce it 'fass-el' not 'fossil!'" they told me. You never know if they are serious. They never are.)

What d'ya mean–let's go?
Let's get outta here.

But you have never really seen Tani and Dran.

Recently, members of the Gillespie County Historical Society had the privilege of experiencing these ladies in their milieu. For the first time in 15 years, Tani and Dran agreed to publicly perform selections from their Broadway play "Two Views."

That is right. Broadway.

Go? We can't get outta here!

The ladies have had a remarkable journey. Several, really. And they continue to live a remarkable life. During a visit in their kitchen at Thistle Hill Manor, I had a tantalizing peek behind the curtain of their careers. For two hours, they teased me with hints of acting with Olivier, starring on Broadway, lunches with T.S. Elliot and travels with Dag Hammarskjold, and covers of *Life* magazine.

Well, then, move over.
I am over.
Well, move over-er!

But they do not wish to dwell on dramas done. In 1993, they decided to turn their backs on that part of their life. They came to the hill country, shedding like serpent skins the idolatry, sycophants, and egos.

I'm hitting the wall, as it is.
So am I.

Did I mention they are twins?
"We are poets," Tani said. "Actually, Dran is prose, I am poetry."

I wonder what's happened to us.

They began weaving a new life. Literally. Creating wool pots from whole cloth and handspun wool.
Even in their existential exile, the universe dared not make them invisible. Draped in flowing dress, scarved and bejeweled, they move through the produce section with grace and "alacrity" (to use some of their own stage direction). They speak with cut and culture, they touch, they listen. They find your eye. They finish each other's sentences. They breathe!

I think we've grown.
Grown? What does that mean?
I don't know–grown–my head's bigger than it used to be.

They discuss for several minutes whether the word "elevate" or "inspire" is the correct verb I should use to describe the effect of their performance. They engage you–you become a third of their "*Two Views*."

You're weird.

They have brilliance, without the glare. As I exited my car, I was listening to opera. "What," I ask the ladies as they come to welcome me to Thistle Hill, "is the song that opens the third act of *Rigoletto*?"

"*La donna è mobile!*" they warble in simultaneous exultation. They begin to sing it.

By the way–your elbow is in my rib again–okay?
Oh, sure. That better?

How can one describe a presence? Naturally, they do it best themselves.

"...actresses and smartasses."

*I've got great news! I can see the way outta here!**

*Excerpts from "Two Views" by and with Dran Hamilton and Tani Guthrie. Used with permission.
Feb 18, 2009

Jay Nash: Thunder Heart

The melodies dip and soar. Sinuous tones evoke the spirit of the sotol and echo the suffering of the soul. If prayer were an instrument, it would be the Native American flute.

It is hard to believe these haunting notes speak from an instrument made and played by a man who only five years ago was paralyzed from the neck down.

But as Jay Nash lay flat on his back, immobilized from a job injury and surgery that for a year left him with no feeling or movement below his chest, the ancient instrument became his lifeline to normalcy.

It had been only a short while before that his friend John Dumas had introduced Nash to the Native American flute during a visit to Sedona, Arizona.

"It literally captivated my soul," Nash recalled. "I told John I would be back in one year and be as good as he was. He laughed, but I worked a year, came back and played with him just as if I'd played it all my life."

Dumas was so impressed that he spent a week teaching Nash the art of making flutes.

Then Nash's world changed. The day before his second surgery, Nash was playing the flute when he had a premonition.

"I told my wife that I had a bad feeling," he admitted. "I said, 'I don't think I'll be playing this flute again.'"

He awakened in the recovery room to the bitter realization he was paralyzed. It was his wife, Lauren, who placed the flute in his hand. Nash cradled the instrument, then looked at his doctor and announced, "This is what is going to make me better."

And it did. As he lay there unable to move, Nash listened to flute music.

"I would close my eyes and remember how to play it," he explained. Nash's "remembering" turned out to be the key to finding his way back.

"Everything in life is controlled by past experience, by how we remember," he said. "That's how I taught myself to walk again. I remembered how to walk. It is as if you turn off the lights at night and try to walk around. You can do it."

Nash used this same "memory" to play the flute again. While Nash can now walk and function normally, he requires constant medication to combat excruciating pain. Incredibly, Nash's fingers are still numb. He literally cannot feel the holes of the flute.

"But I can remember where they are in my mind, how they feel, and where they are," he said.

It is no exaggeration to say the flute saved his life.

"The flute kept me active and my mind going," Nash said, who now builds flutes in his workshop south of Fredericksburg. "This helps take my mind off the pain. It sends me to a place of tranquility."

Nash uses sotol, yucca, bamboo, walnut, cedar, and redwood to create beautiful looking and sounding instruments.

"Flutes possess their own spirit," he said. "Some are made of bamboo that has lived its life cycle. Making a flute is taking a thing that is dead, and giving it life again. Some people drive by a stand of bamboo and see a plant. I drive by and see music."

Nash does offer his flutes for sale, but admits it is an emotional business.

"I have a hard time letting go of any flute I make," he said. "I fall in love with every one."

When he is convinced to part with one, the price ranges from $55 to more than $500, depending on the wood, time involved, and intricacy of the carving. He can turn out several bamboo flutes a day, or spend four days creating a bird head flute.

"It depends on how I feel," he said, noting that he sometimes stops to play a flute just so he can escape the pain of working on it.

Nash captured the healing spirit of the instrument in his first CD *Thunder Heart*.

"Nothing was written–everything I play is from the heart,' he said. "Everything you hear on the CD happened right there. It is so amazing. To me that's the ultimate way to make music–all from the heart."

Ultimately, it's the metaphysical rather than physical aspect of the instrument that inspires Nash to go on living, making flutes, and playing music.

"To me it's a miracle–a gift from God," he said. "This has given me a way to express what I experienced. I want to share my story, to give encouragement. God has given me a gift to share. With the flute I can introduce people to different ways of praying."

May 10, 2006

Pickup Truck, Texas

Magnolia Thunder Blossom was just destined to be part of Luckenbach.

Growing up in Alabama–before she became Magnolia–Maggie Montgomery marched to her own thunder.

"I was a pretty rebellious teenager," she said. "I always sang, that kind of set me apart. It was the 60s, there were hippies, and everybody was playing guitar."

She wanted to play music, but she couldn't find a fit.

"In Alabama all you heard was bluegrass," she explained. "That was people standing around in a circle, tapping their feet, with no expression on their faces, playing the same thing over and over."

Montgomery had some friends who were in love with Texas. They told her about the hill country, Luckenbach, and Hondo. They told her to go–just go.

"I wanted to drink a Lone Star beer and be part of the music scene," she said. So in 1975, she went. "I drove straight to Luckenbach, and sure enough met Hondo."

As soon as she saw the place, she became "completely hooked."

Luckenbach became hooked on Maggie Montgomery too. Over the intervening decades, Montgomery has woven herself into the tapestry of that legendary town. She became Magnolia Thunder Blossom, regular contributor to the Luckenbach Moon, songwriter, picker, and a founder of the Luckenbach Ladies Lynching League Chili Cookoff Team. Her song *Pickup Truck, Texas* was recorded by Gary P. Nunn, and of course, her son who followed her to Luckenbach a few years later as a teenager, became Monte Montgomery, guitar legend.

But the title she is most proud of came from Hondo.

"Hondo named me the Luckenbach Songbird," she said, adding, "People around here are real big on titles, whether they earned them or not."

With all her accomplishments, she considers herself most of all a songwriter. "If they said all songwriters move to the left, I moved to the left."

Maggie now lives just a pickup ride from Luckenbach at the one-house town of Banker Smith (Montiac World Headquarters). She just finished recording her first CD. It was a long, long labor of love that she just never seemed to get around to finishing.

"It took forever to get Monte to find the time to do it," she said. "We were shopping studios to do it. I finally booked a studio in Austin at 10:30 at night. Monte said, Mom, this is not what you want to do. He said let's just do it with you and me like we used to."

So one day in Monte's living room, using two mics and two guitars, the duo knocked it out in 10 hours. The result is *Pickup Truck, Texas*, with Maggie Montgomery singing her songs backed up by her very special guest guitarist.

The only "produced" song is a redo of *Pickup Truck, Texas* that they recorded at Arlen Studio with the help of the Banker Smith Abnormal Fishing Tackle Choir providing background voices.

The result is pure Maggie.

"Monte said it sounds like you are singing on the back porch or around the campfire," she said. "People think since it's Monte's mom, it will be rocking. But it's more like rocking chair."

They just started playing, left in the little comments, and sometimes made it up as they went.

"We were amazed we remembered every single note and every single word, just like we used to play it," Montgomery said. "It sounds like back when I was the star!"

Maggie loves to recount how Monte started out next to her, strumming his guitar.

"One night he said, I think I can play some lead. I said, go for it.

Then he started playing my songs, then he started playing his own set, then he got gigs on his own." She laughed. "Now he is in Italy playing for thousands and I'm still in Banker Smith. But I'm just as happy sitting here at Banker Smith as he is traveling the world."

One night he called her from Nashville and she asked what he was doing.

"He said he was in the hotel, waiting for a limo to pick him up to take him to the recording studio. I said I'm waiting to see if my car will start!"

Maggie's self-deprecating humor is part of her appeal, along with her twisted view on the world and her joy in making music. It is hard to see where the real Maggie stops and Magnolia begins. It's all the same to her.

"This is really and truly me–I couldn't make that kind of stuff up!"

So what's next? More music, of course.

"I have a whole passel of songs I haven't recorded, so I may do more. Just now I'm trying to figure out what I'm going to wear when Monte plays for the Queen at Albert Hall."

Seems to me he has already played for a queen at Luckenbach Dance Hall.

Jan 20, 2010

Turkey Baster: Out of the Kitchen

There was a new grease slinger in town.

He pulled up to the local speakeasy. Walked in carrying a violin case. A very, very tiny violin case.

He sized up the musicians on stage, then placed his violin case on the glass-topped table. Experienced fingers unlatched the catches and lifted the lid. Inside lay his instrument. Three of them, actually.

Turkey basters. All loaded, tuned, and ready to blow.

"I'm Ray Sanders. I play the turkey baster. And I'm going to play a song for you."

That is how the world was introduced to the foremost authority on performing with the turkey baster.

The Bryan, Texas, band teacher first picked up the "instrument" about 10 years ago.

"I'm often asked how I came to play the baster," he explained. "I have several stories. But the true story is that I was on a mission trip in charge of music and also working in the kitchen. One little girl said, what are you going to do–play the spoons? So I said something smart back: No, I'm going to play the turkey baster."

So he took it out of the drawer, and launched his unlikely career.

Sanders started playing simple tunes such as *Jesus Loves Me* and *Beethoven's Ninth*. This actually works, he realized. So he moved on to the *William Tell Overture, Stars and Stripes Forever* (on piccolo baster), and his signature piece–*Flight of the Bumblebee*.

Success came literally overnight. He saw a small blurb in his local newspaper that said, "Talent needed."

"I said, hey, that's me! I have talent."

So he set up a camera, dressed in a dirty T-shirt, affected a thick, hick accent, and submitted a song.

To his surprise, they called him back.

"They called and said, we've been having a ball watching your tape, and we want you to be on our telethon. I said, OK, I'll come over."

To Sanders' bigger surprise, they said, no, this is the MDA Telethon and we want you to come to Los Angeles. They flew him out to the show, where he appeared with the Muppets. Three weeks later, he was featured on Stupid Human Tricks on *The Late Show with David Letterman* in New York.

"In one month I went coast to coast playing a kitchen utensil," he said, shaking his head.

Sanders picks up his instrument and begins playing his set. So many people asked him questions, he began weaving his answers in between songs:

"The most pure, natural sounds are produced with warm turkey grease. However, that does get a little foul smelling. I use peach tea. People can see it, and it works better if I need to tune the instrument." (he swallows a mouthful as the audience goes, "Eeeewww!")

"Some say the turkey baster is not a musical instrument. I say if you play music on it, it's an instrument."

"Musical history is unclear whether anybody played it or nobody admitted playing it. I can understand that because I played about a year before I came out of the kitchen."

"It takes such little movement squeezing the bulb, that you must have a good ear. I do; I can hear when I play the wrong notes."

"If I'm nervous, that's vibrato."

"Give me a break; I'm playing a kitchen utensil here."

"Sometimes I get paid one thousand dollars; sometimes I get paid one hundred dollars; sometimes I get chicken-fried steak."

"Like any musical talent it is a wonderful gift from God; but I'm not trying to make it look like I'm blaming God."

Behind the bluster, Sanders admits to an ulterior motive.

"I promote good music; I promote school music. School music is on the fringe of getting cut out. Then where will our musicians and composers come from? That is my motive, but this is fun, and it should be fun for the listener."

Sanders packed up his basters and picked up the violin case. As he headed for his car, he paused, and looked back at the bemused crowd.

"I'm not a geek," he said softly. "I'm just a musician."

July 27, 2011

Sunshine the Clown

It's the kind of store you loved to go into when you were a kid.

There is the fake fly in the ice cube, the spilled coffee, the finger-shaped nose hair trimmer, a plastic rat, and the doormat that read, "Come Back With a Warrant." And then there are the classics: the handshake buzzer, fake vomit, and, of course, the rubber chicken.

Interestingly, the day I was in the Old Thyme Fun Shop on Main Street it wasn't kids buying the hillbilly teeth and rolling eyeballs. Instead, a steady stream of giggling grownups hauled away bags of fake bagels with the cockroach, and piles of T-shirts with naughty messages.

Ruling this kingdom of kitsch is Shannon Anderson, aka Sunshine the Clown.

It is amazing that Anderson is in the clown business at all. She didn't start clowning until 15 years ago, and she admits it was "strictly a financial decision."

"When I moved to Fredericksburg, I wondered what do I already know how to do to make a living?" she said. "Well, I already know magic, and I know balloons... I'll be a clown!"

Her first attempt at clowning was not much fun. In fact, she called it a "disaster."

"I was at this house full of fifth-graders, and they had every video game and a big screen TV, and here's this clown doing magic tricks,"

she recalled. "All of them were saying 'when are you going to leave?'"
She chuckled. "I said, 'Now! Close your eyes and count to 10,' and I
was out the door! I went home and said I'm never doing this again!
Kids are mean!"

Luckily, Anderson couldn't walk away from her clowning career as
easy as that. She already had another gig booked.

She decided that to be funny, she would have to work at it. So she
studied other clowns, read books and watched tapes, and attended
conventions to learn the art of the clown.

"Some people think anybody can do it; you just slap on some makeup and funny clothes," she said. "It's not that way. There really is an
art to it."

Anderson has progressed so far she recently traveled to Russia with
Patch Adams, the doctor immortalized in a movie for his work using
clown techniques for healing.

That was quite an adventure, even for an extrovert like Anderson.
Her group made the entire Russia trip "in clown"–in makeup and
costume.

"That was my biggest fear–flying in clown," she said. "Now I think
that is the only way to travel! People came up and talked to you. I got
proposed to. One lady gave me 20 bucks on the shuttle bus to take to
Russia to do something for the kids." She laughed at the memory.

Anderson pointed out that the clowning she did in Russia was in every sense miles away from going to people's houses to entertain them.
She visited kids in hospitals and orphanages, trying to bring them to a
more pleasant place.

"We were trying to connect with them and create a moment where
their reality was different," she said. "Where they have reckless laughter instead of not enough food."

Anderson understands the depth of that pain. After losing her infant
son, Aaron, eight years ago, Sunshine helped heal her.

"It was so much easier to be Sunshine than it was to be Shannon,"
she recalled. "When people came up and asked, 'how are you,' I could
say, 'she's okay,' but this other girl is not. It was difficult, but I looked
forward to being Sunshine as much as I could. It really helped me a
lot."

Today she sees her son in every child's eyes, connecting her with
every child on the planet.

"I just have this thing with kids," she said. "I would rather deal with
children than adults, personally. It's for real, there are no games or
manipulation."

She paused to show a customer how to perform the national anthem on a whoopee cushion. Obviously, clowning will always be part of Anderson's life.

"Laughter is therapeutic, it shakes up all your organs and makes a chemical reaction in your body that no drug can replace," she said. "Letting yourself play as an adult is one of the greatest things we can do for ourselves in this hectic, serious world. There's humor in everything, like it or not."

April 25, 2007

Galevis

Elvis may be dead. But he still plays Fredericksburg.

On a special night, somewhere along the widest Main Street in Texas, you might be fortunate enough to hear The King reprising his hits for townspeople and travelers.

Like the Ghost Riders in the Sky, the Flying Dutchmen, and the Lost Boys, Elvis Presley refuses to go gently into that dark night. His Fredericksburg incarnation is "Gale-vis," a wigged and caped, sequin jump-suited version of the god of rock and roll. I can't really tell you where and when Galevis appears. His performances are ethereal, befitting the Ghost of Graceland. But I was fortunate enough to track him down for an interview one recent misty night.

Q: I thought you were dead.

Galevis: I was. But it got boring. You know they sing about "rock and roll heaven," but it isn't all heavenly. All the best dead musicians aren't there, if you know what I mean...

Q: Many myths have arisen since you left us. What misconceptions do people still have about you?

Galevis: The clothes. I don't unnerstand why they think I should still wear polyester jump suits with sequins, 30 years after that went out of style. I really prefer natural fibers. And everyone portrays me as being fat. To tell the truth, I lost a lot of weight after I died.

Q: What is the hardest part of being an icon?

Galevis: The hardest part is that I can't go into a Subway without my picture showing up on the cover of Star magazine. You'd think a guy could enjoy the occasional meatball sandwich without having to hide behind a wig, high collar, cape, and dark glasses. Of course, that's what I wear all the time, anyway.

Q: How has the music changed since you "left the building?"

Galevis: Today's music is just unmelodic noise with insipid lyrics. Where are the great songs with textured storytelling and complex musical arrangements like Hound Dog and Jailhouse Rock? Those are classics, man.

Q: Have you been playing much in the past 30 years?

Galevis: Actually, we get the old Sun Records gang together for the occasional celestial clambake–Carl, Johnny, Roy, and me. Waiting on old Jerry Lee to show up–the way he lived we are surprised we've had to wait this long.

Q: Any plans for another comeback?

Galevis: I applied for a part in this new Rock Opry coming to town, but they already had an Elvis.

Q: Anything you want to say to your loyal fans?

Galevis eased himself out of his seat, adjusted his cape, and headed for the stage. He paused and turned, and gave me a wink.

"Tell them...," he said, his lip drawn up in that Elvis sneer, "tell them... it feels good to crawl out of your hole every once in awhile and get all shook up."

The King is dead. Long live the King.

March 28, 2007

4 Proches: All for One

When I was in my early 20s, I wanted to be in a band so badly that I forced my little brothers to play. I showed one a few bass licks, and got my youngest brother to play drums. Since drums were my instrument, I had to learn some guitar just so I could still be in the group. It didn't matter what instrument I had to play. I just wanted to play. I figured it was the quickest way I could be popular.

That is sort of how the 4 Proches got their start. Except they possess more talent and embrace higher aspirations.

The 4 Proches are Beecher, 20; Ezra, 17; Liza, 14; and Asa, 10. They are the home-schooled children of Janet and Tom Proche.

All sing and play piano. From there, the instrumentation gets complicated. I think I sorted it out one morning at their practice. Ezra plays banjo. Liza is working on fiddle, and also plays harp, but not in this group. Beecher plays guitar. Six months ago Asa picked up the mandolin because the band needed one, and "it's my size." He also plays djembe and spoons.

They describe their style of music as Southern folk, or bluegrass folk. Think *Wayfaring Stranger*. Clean string accompaniment with full vocal harmonies.

More importantly, the siblings are writing. Beecher usually comes up with the lyrics, then turns them over to Ezra for creating the melody.

"The stuff we are writing still has a folksy attitude," Ezra explained. "More like Alison Krause."

Watching and listening to the 4 Proches perform one afternoon at Hondo's brought out another perspective. From my current perch in life, I am able to relate as much to the "parent" part of having a family band.

My father wanted to play trumpet as a lad, but as spawn of the Depression, he had to work and give the money he made at a grocery store to his family. So when he had kids of his own, he made sure we all had music lessons and instruments. He was our band's biggest supporter, and always sat in the front row, no matter how seedy the club we were playing in.

Similarly, Tom Proche did not have the opportunity to make music growing up. That makes watching his kids perform even more special.

"I always dreamed of being able to pick up a guitar or sit at the piano and play," he said. "But I was busy playing golf, baseball, hunting, fishing, and building things–there wasn't any time for music."

While he never learned to play an instrument, Tom did gain an appreciation of symphonic music, learned about the instruments and composers, and sang in a choir. He passed that love for music along to his children, and made sure they all were able to take music lessons and attend concerts. He finds this role turned out to be more gratifying.

"I couldn't do it, but this is even better," he said. "Now I get to sit and listen to my kids pick up the guitar. It's an even bigger blessing than I could ever imagine." There is an added bonus. "Their music is a blessing to other people, too. They recognize and enjoy that."

Mom also is proud.

"It is just a blast," Janet said. "Because you picture what teenager-hood is going to be like, and you can get scared. But this is pure joy. I am living my total dream. It is incredibly sweet."

The children of course enjoy it most of all, and they have their priorities straight.

"Our first goal is to glorify God," said Ezra. "Under that is to provide great role models for others our age."

Not that they would disdain fame and glory.

"We totally would like that," Beecher said, "but I'm not shooting for fame. I just love to make music. We all do. That is the foundation of it all. And we love to share it with others."

Aug 28, 2013

The Gift of Flute

Virgie Raven Hawk considers the music that sings from her flute as a gift from God. It was a gift she did not open until she turned 50.

That was around 1995, when she retired from the Army. She was at a powwow in Tennessee when she heard the sound of flute. Raven Hawk walked over to compliment the player, unexpectedly opening a new level of spirituality in her own life.

"That lady turned around and said, well ma'am, if you are really interested, you can buy one of my flutes and I'll give you 30 minutes of my time. If I can't get you to play, I'll give you back your money." She laughed. "It was a deal I couldn't refuse!"

Despite the fact that Raven Hawk had never had any musical training, after one-half hour she was playing.

"The spirit moves in mysterious ways," she said. "I was given the gift of flute."

It is a gift the spiritual woman does not carry lightly. Her heritage is Aztec and Wichita, a label that carried a stigma in the previous generation.

"You weren't allowed to speak of that heritage; it caused extreme shame," she said. "You were lower than dirt."

But her father had given her another gift–the gift of carving in wood and stone. That ability not only helped heal her, it helped maintain her heritage.

"My father would allow me to come into his workshop where he would tell stories of his people," she remembered. "We were never allowed to speak of it in the house... never."

After 23 years of active duty, a spinal injury ended her military career and left her paralyzed.

"I was angry with life, I had a broken back, and no use of my legs," she said. After surgery, she was able to walk again. "I said, well, Creator, I know you are calling me for something. My recovery was to stop being angry with God."

Raven Hawk started doing what her father had shown her earlier in life–she carved, showing her work at powwows. With her partner, Debbie Drum Hawk, she now does spiritual work, teaching the old ways, the ways of drumming circles, lodges, and spirit walks.

"When people have already lost themselves from God, we try to find them an easier way to seek creation."

But for Raven Hawk, the flute is her most powerful gift.

"I think it is more spiritual–it touches their hearts when they hear and see it and be next to it," she said. "When I hold a drumming circle and finish with flute, it sends them to another place. And it is their place, not mine... it is their place."

She picks up a flute and fingers it silently.

"I don't know where the music comes from," she said, gazing at the slender instrument. "I can sit here and you can ask me to play each and everyone of these flutes, and they will all be different and I don't know why. If you ask me to play something from my CD, I'll say I can't. But something comes forth."

Like her Wichita heritage, the playing has come full circle.

"People ask do I give lessons," she said. "I do. How much do you charge? I tell them I cannot charge for a gift that was free."

"When you are given a gift like this you have no choice but to turn around and offer it to others. If you keep it, it is just going to walk away from you."

And she begins to play.

June 18, 2008

The Pipes Are Calling

Whenever I have needed an obtuse musical reference I have called upon the bagpipe, figuring there were no Scottish Highlanders in the Texas hills to take offense.

I stand corrected, and duly admonished, for now we have an authentic piper in our midst.

Ian Blackie, who moved to Fredericksburg last May, is a native of New Zealand. While that country is 12,000 miles from Scotland–traditional home of the bagpipe–Blackie boasts proud Scottish roots from his grandparents, who influenced his love for the instrument he has played for 40 years. New Zealand apparently has a rich tradition for Scottish music.

"I grew up in a very small town one-third the size of Fredericksburg," he noted. "Even though it was a small community, it had its own pipe band. At one point there were more pipe bands in New Zealand than in Scotland."

He pointed out the historical connection between Scotland and Texas, starting with the 30 Scots who fought in the Battle of the Alamo to the more than half of all Texas counties named for Scots. Some linguists even maintain that the Texan phrase "y'all" evolved from Gaelic. In spite of the shared history, Blackie is aware of America's ambivalence toward the traditional Scottish instrument.

"Some of that distaste is deserved because some people who play bagpipes here don't play it well," he said. "I like to play the very best I can so they get a good impression of the instrument."

Appreciation of the pipes is an elusive quality. Bagpipes were woven into the lives and culture of Europe in the 16th and 17th centuries. They were the centerpiece of weddings and religious festivals, and led British military forces into battle right up to World War II. But due to their limited musical range, they gradually fell out of favor, a trend that continues to the present day.

What does Blackie consider to be the true beauty of bagpipes?

"It is difficult to answer, because the sound of the instrument and of a good band gets my attention every time. I have been doing it for so long, that it's part of me, I guess. But it is also cultural. One of the things I do when I teach is to make sure the student has an understanding not only of the history of the instrument, but also of the music itself. It is very rich."

Blackie, who runs a small marketing company, turns to marketing when he performs at special occasions. He likes to share some history of the instrument, explain how it works, and answer questions about the music.

"I have interest in getting involved in the community as far as music, whether teaching or playing, whatever it might be," said Blackie. "But the focus is always on the bagpipes."

The pipes, the pipes are calling.

March 12, 2008

Cowboy Doug

I first encountered Cowboy Doug Davis hanging out at Hondo's. In his jeans and boots, with sweat-stained cowboy hat framing his etched, bearded face, he could have walked off the set of a western movie. Turns out, he did. He played a part in the movie *American Outlaws* that was filmed in Austin.

"There wasn't much acting to it," he offered. "Mostly just standing around. I did have a speaking part." He worked his face into character, then cupped his hand to his mouth and yelled, "Estan escapando!"

Besides acting, Cowboy Doug has been a camp cook, vacuum cleaner salesman, oil field roughneck, professional gunfighter, bartender, and musician. I heard him accompanying champion fiddler Bart Trotter one recent Sunday morning for a Windows on Texas event.

His acoustic rhythm guitar work is deceptively steady western swing style. Deceptive, because he makes it look easy. He is doing the work of an entire band, laying down a solid rhythm, with moving bass line, and changing jazz chords on every beat.

"And that was early in the morning," he added with a grin. "Ever since I was a little kid, I've been making music of some sort or another. I started playing guitar around age 12. I also played trumpet in the school band and sang in the choir at church."

Cowboy Doug grew up in Virginia, but sounds more Texan than most Texans sound. ("I've now lived in Texas longer than I lived in Virginia," he explained. "A lot of the early Texas Rangers were from Virginia; I figure I'm carrying on the tradition of Virginians with sense enough to move to Texas.") He got to Texas through Nashville, where he first tried to find fame and fortune.

"When that didn't work out, we heard Austin was cool, so we went to Austin," he said. There he met up with a group of old-time western swing musicians. "That's where I saw how all that moving chord work was done."

Talking to Cowboy Doug, you notice that every answer holds a nugget of information about another fascinating part of his life. It's like finding gold in a pan of pebbles.

For example:

"I met Bart when I was on a cross-country horse trip," Cowboy Doug said. "We were resting our horses in Ruidosa, and this guy said you got to hear this band that's playing out at the Flying J. We got out there and Bart was playing fiddle with a guy that wasn't backing him up the way I thought he should. I asked if he'd mind if I picked one with him. We launched into something and hit it off from the first note."

Nugget: Cross-country horse trip?

"A lady I know started riding a horse from Terlingua," he explained. "I was giving her vehicle support until she reached the Guadalupe Mountains. Then I left my car there and bought a horse and rode the rest of the way to Santa Fe with her. It took us two or three months." He laughed. "It just seemed like the thing to do."

Nugget: Living in Terlingua?

"I took two weeks off to play music for the chili cookoff there," he said. "I got back 11 years later. In Terlingua, I did a lot of pack trips and dude wrangling."

Nugget: Dude wrangling?

"I worked on lot of ranches and racetracks, including Belmont Park and Churchill Downs," he went on. "I was an exercise boy and a groom."

So how did Cowboy Doug the cowboy decide to become Cowboy Doug the guitar player?

"I wasn't really trying to make a living at music then, but every once in a while I got a job that paid so good it spoiled me for regular work," he said. "Ha ha!"

Even though he's not a writer of songs ("every time I start one, it seems like someone else already wrote it"), Cowboy Doug has burnished his nuggets of experience into cowboy logic.

"If I had to boil it down, I guess, I'd say I wouldn't do anything for money that I wouldn't do for free if I was independently wealthy."

So that means money is not important?

"Nope. It means I'm broke all the time."

So he wouldn't give up music to, say... work in a bank? His response was not a surprise.

"Actually, I did work in a bank while I was in high school," he said. "The thing is, I'm so crippled up now, I can't work cowboying. At this point, music is about all I can do that pays anything, that I can do sitting down."

Feb 7, 2007

Polkamatics

We don't practice.
We don't play any place that doesn't serve beer.
We don't wear leather pants.

So goes the credo of the Polkamatics, a Fredericksburg "band" that gets together only one time a year to play for Oktoberfest.

Formed of remnants of assorted local musical entities (such as the We'd Rather Not Be Marching Band and the B.S. Band), the Polkamatics helped close out (fittingly) this year's Oktoberfest.

When Bill Smallwood, de facto leader of the group ("I own the sound system") introduced the group, he noted with pride that "Our members are conscious of our rules."

"We're conscious?" someone yelled from the tuba section.

I had the pleasure of sitting in with the group ("Hey, can you come play... we need all the help we can get") this year.

It was an interesting experience.

We were well into our first half-hour polka medley and the audience was still there, though they sat with jaws agape and brows knitted. You see, the brilliance of the Polkamatics approach to music is not immediately evident to first-time listeners.

For one thing, every song begins and ends with a lengthy, spirited drum cadence. Lengthy, because it allows time for band members to find the music (or in some cases, pass the music down to the trombone section); spirited, because the band boasts two drummers. They used to have three.

"We apologize for our rhythm being off tonight, but we lost our conductor and one of our drummers this year. Otherwise, we are out of excuses."

The repertoire is wide-ranging. The first set included both *Hey Good Looking* and the *She's Too Fat Polka*.

"We always like to announce the names of our songs first, in case someone knows these and might not recognize them."

The band is so large–it seemed to fluctuate between 16 and 19 players during the gig–that members can take bathroom breaks in shifts without the band having to stop playing, or the audience noticing.

The frequent trips to the bathroom might be a result of the constant traffic between the bandstand and the bar. Midway through the set, it looked like an anthill, as fans shuttled frosty beverages from the taps to the lips of thirsty horn players.

Yes, there are fans. Their reaction to a Polkamatics concert is akin to watching a car accident–discomforting, but you just can't look away.

Eventually, they seemed to get it. A few even danced, though keeping their distance from the bandstand. One brave couple came up and asked if the Polkamatics had a CD.

"Are you kidding? Who'd record this stuff?"

The show turned out to be the perfect way to close out Oktoberfest. The band ended most of the numbers at the same time and in the same key, and when we ran out of songs, no one minded (or realized) that we repeated the first half-hour.

"We've had many requests, but we are going to keep playing anyway."

If you are skeptical of this account, just show up next year and hear the Polkamatics for yourself.

Just look for the band that's not wearing leather pants (and pray they are wearing some sort of pants).

"By the way... how do you think this Oktoberfest thing is working out? Maybe they ought to try it again next year."

Nov 8, 2006

Duncan Holmes and Lucky

Duncan Holmes
Many Styles; One Message

You've heard him play hymns in church, rock and roll at festivals, swing at a dance hall, jazz in a lounge, and even show tunes at school.

Duncan Holmes can play the piano in every style with the same aplomb and energy. But the music genre matters less than his musical message.

"The most important thing I want to communicate is that there is more to this life than living and dying, eating and eliminating," Holmes said. "God created us to have a purpose. I want to convey that in my music and what I do in my life. That is why I do what I do. I try to keep that uppermost in my mind every day."

His academic pedigree includes degrees from the Shenandoah Conservatory of Music and the University of North Texas. While in prep school, he formed "The Swingin' Teens" and over the years toured and played at numerous jazz festivals and performance halls, as well as community churches.

Blind from birth, Holmes found inspiration in music at an early age.

"I was fortunate to grow up in a family of music lovers," Holmes said. "We had the radio and record player going all the time."

Holmes remembers the exact moment he decided to make music his career.

"My family took me to listen to Roger Williams when I was in seventh grade," he said. "I had never heard a live, professional pianist before. Right then I knew what I wanted to do."

What he wanted to do was make music "my life and my livelihood."

It was in 1986 that he and his wife, Sharon, were able to turn Fredericksburg from their "great escape" to their permanent home, moving here from Denton.

"I thought 'what is a blind guy going to do in Fredericksburg," he said. "But then I thought, 'what am I doing where I am?'"

So Sharon began teaching kindergarten, and Duncan pursued his music.

Holmes plays regularly at the Evangelical Free Church, and he is sought after around the country to share his message of music and Christian message in churches, schools, and prisons. He also performs at the Hangar Hotel, both solo and with a small combo.

Holmes is bemused by curiosity about his blindness.

"People must bear in mind not every blind person is a musician," he said. "I know blind people who can't carry a tune, who may not even like music. I just happen to be a person who is blind and who loves music."

In fact, Holmes' ultimate message transcends the physical world. Even when playing jazz in a lounge, he enjoys slipping in songs with a message of faith, such as *Amazing Grace* or *How Great Thou Art*.

"I know not everyone can come to the church," he said. "If I can't say it I want it to come through in my music. I want them to know from Whom the glory really comes. I try to be as consistent as possible, both playing at the club and at the church. If I can't say it, I'll play it."

Oct 18, 2006

Seeking His Voice

"I am about fiddling."

If Gale Reddick were a company, that would be his mission statement.

Reddick, who performs at least 30 hours a week and practices many hours more, has overcome some homegrown odds to reach his goals.

Born in Fredericksburg and raised around Harper, Reddick remembers wanting a fiddle at the age of six. But in small town Texas in the 1950s, scraping out music was not a viable career choice.

"Musicians were seen as derelicts," Reddick recalled. "It was not what you would consider a desirable lifestyle at that time."

Reddick also ran up against a perception that musical talent was something "you were born with."

"The attitude was that if you are gifted, you can play music," he said. "If you don't have the gift, you can't. I'm still struggling with this. There are people who have the gift. I know I never will have it."

Reddick made up for it, ironically using skills he learned in his early life.

"What I lacked in raw talent, I made up with practice, stamina, work, determination, and... and..."

He searched for the right word.

"... and just plain stubbornness," he finally said. "That's all I've really got and I'm running with it."

The bug never left him, but Reddick had to wait until he was 30 before he got his fingers on his first serious fiddle. He accepted an offer of a free lesson from a member of the San Antonio symphony. That was all it took.

"I went and started taking lessons everywhere I could," he said. "It was so good to finally play."

"To me, the only definition of talent is desire," Reddick said. "How bad do you really want to do this and keep going with all the odds against you?"

After 30 years of fiddling, Reddick continues his quest to learn everything about the instrument, while trying to discover that thing "that connects us to the universe."

"My mission is to find my voice," he said. "I want to find a delivery that's mine, that is distinctive and unique, and not in a vain way. I really want people to say 'I've got my own voice, too.'"

Reddick's musical voice revolves around a unique style of playing that he dubs "triple stops." In violin lexicon, double stops are the technique of bowing two adjacent strings simultaneously. This usually creates two-part harmony or sometimes doubling of the same note. Reddick had the idea of adding his voice to create a third part. His original songs are made of a melody he sings while simultaneously playing two harmony parts on the violin. It creates a full sound, and is very challenging to perform. He has worked for years to perfect the technique, and is now putting the finishing touches on 45 original songs which he will include in a book.

"I call them 'uplifting meditations,'" he said. Each piece includes lyrics, and the tunes are designed to encourage the violinist to incorporate his singing voice while playing the instrument.

The boy who was told he would never play an instrument now performs five days a week and teaches guitar and violin whenever he's not on stage.

How will he know his mission is accomplished?

"If I ever get it right, I want to be like Elijah and get carried away in a chariot to the next realm," he said. "But that's if I ever get it right. I'll probably die trying."

Nov 2, 2005

Mariachi, Morquecho-style

The guitar hung tantalizingly out of reach.

Five-year-old Fritz Morquecho would sit across the bed each week while his brother had his guitar lesson, then watch wistfully as the older boy carefully returned the shiny new instrument to its perch high on the wall.

The temptation was finally too much for little Fritz. He figured out how to push a chair against the wall and climb up to get that guitar. Recalling what the teacher had shown his brother, Morquecho began practicing in secret.

"Learning music has never been difficult for me," Morquecho said.

"I could hear a chord and then play it."

He played it so much he began leaving scratches on the surface.

"My brother finally said I had scratched it so bad, he just gave it to me," Morquecho recalled, laughing.

That was the start of a lifelong musical career that's taken him through the worlds of Texas and Tejano music.

By the time he started school, he was entertaining his classmates with music. At age 7, Morquecho and a friend were good enough to play little jobs for Josefina "Chata" Torres, who owned the popular Tortilla Factory that stood behind the HEB grocery store in Kerrville.

"We would dress up in mariachi outfits and play and sing," he recalled. In the late 1940s Fritz even performed with Tejano music pioneer Rosita Fernandez–la Rosa de San Antonio–who died recently.

At 14, Morquecho wrapped his arms around his first true love–the accordion.

"I had an uncle who played the button accordion," he said. "He came to visit one time, and stayed up until 4 a.m., talking and showing me how it worked."

By 7 a.m. Fritz could play his first song–*La Margarita*.

"The bug caught me then," he said. For the next six weeks, young Morquecho took off to pick cotton, just to earn enough money to buy his first real accordion.

Morquecho performed throughout the 1950s as The Three Aces, playing dance halls and community centers. In the 1960s, Morquecho's children were old enough to join him and they became the Morquecho Family band.

By the late 1970s, Morquecho formed Mariachi de Kerrville, the group he continues to front. It includes his cousin Joe on guitar, Manuel Sanchez on guitar, Sam Rios on acoustic bass, and Gilbert Morales on vihuela.

These days, Morquecho is still entertaining his friends. He plays regularly at school suppers and family nights. He is a popular performer in clubs and concerts. He takes his accordion onstage with bluegrass, blues, and jazz groups. When a zydeco band performed at one of the Roots concerts, Morquecho was backstage getting them to show him how to coax that deep swamp sound out of his 3-row button accordion. I have even heard the mariachi maestro playing a Russian folk song.

Morquecho's wide interests are evident in his CD *Fritz & Friends*. Selections include Tejano ballads, German polkas, and cowboy cumbias.

"I put a little bit of everything on my CD," he explained. "When you grow up in Texas, you hear all kinds of songs. When someone from the audience would come up and ask for a country song, if we didn't know it, by the next gig it was ready. I haven't done just mariachi all my life!"

Morquecho, who is a retired barber, has no plans to slow down. He still gives accordion lessons and stays "fairly busy," he said. "I'm going to keep on playing as long as I can drive to the gigs."

In fact, a few years ago, he began to learn the violin. And he didn't have to climb the wall to get at it.

May 24, 2006

Dick Walker:
Play a Little Longer

Have you ever been to a funeral that you didn't want to end?
Dick Walker is that good.

The funeral was an intimate service in a small church in Kingsland.
After the praying and the remembering, Walker picked up his bow
and began playing the violin (accompanied by Tim Porter on acoustic guitar–another incredible musician). The setting, the mood, and
the exquisite taste and tone that came from two men playing stringed
instruments was mesmerizing. I was reluctant to let the bittersweet
moment go.

Now living in Leakey ("...one of the garden spots in Texas–what a
fortunate man I was that my wife happened to be raised there"), Walker
was born in Denver and raised "surrounded by Baptist preachers and

fiddle players."

"I grew up knowing what the fiddle was supposed to sound like," he said. "My family wanted me to be the one who would do it right."

So Walker took lessons from age 7 to 18. Unfortunately, the boy and his father did not see eye to eye, leading the young musician to announce "I wasn't going to play the fiddle anymore, and I never touched it once for 20 years."

But Walker couldn't walk away that easily.

"In 1978, I hung up law enforcement. I was wondering what I was going to do with myself, when music came back into my life," he said. It came back with a passion. He earned a master's degree and did graduate work in violin performance. "Nothing has ever consumed me like playing the violin. It's not that I'm obsessed with it, it just happens to be the one thing in life that I'm damned good at."

By 1989, Walker had moved to Texas permanently. He performs regularly with Geronimo Trevino III, and also teaches, something he has had to acquire a taste for doing.

"When I first started teaching I didn't like it all," he said. "Being an introvert, I just wanted to stay in my own bubble. I've come to find out that teaching people to play violin is a relationship I build, not only with my students, but also with the people around them."

But with Walker, everything comes back to his relationship to the violin.

"I'll be 68 this year, and for the first time in my life I'm starting to say I'll be 70," he said. "I had a really good friend who got to this age long before I did. He said, you know when you get to my age, you are going to need a reason to get out of bed in the morning. For me, that is music."

As the Dick Walker Trio (with Porter and Gary Hatch on upright bass), he has some strong opinions on how a performance should go.

"At the beginning of our concert, I take a few minutes to talk, because when we start playing, I probably won't say another word," Walker said. "I tell the audience up front there are two things we are going to do. One, I want you to leave here wishing I'd have turned up the sound system. Two, I want you leaving here wishing I'd have stayed longer."

Even if he happens to be playing at a funeral.

Jan 3, 2007

Struck by a Bolt of Music

One fine summer Saturday I decided to play tourist in my own town, and went for a stroll along Main Street. Always alert for interesting music, I detected the distinctive drone of a button accordion through the rumble of traffic and shuffling of shoppers.

Tucked in the courtyard of the former Keidel Hospital, Terry Theis played a German waltz for curious kids and parents willing to pause in their pursuit of the perfect gewgaw.

The Texas native was the vision of a gypsy accordionista, sporting a mustache and beret with a button declaring "I'm a Polkaholic."

Until about three years ago, Theis never considered himself musical at all. He spent 20 years as a gun engraver, frequently exhibiting his skill at the Texas Folklife Festival in San Antonio.

In fact it was there that Theis was first "struck by a bolt of music."

"I heard some conjunto players at the Folklife Festival, then went to the annual accordion fest at La Villita," he recalled. "It was obvious–I walked out of there knowing that's what I need to be doing."

Acknowledging that he is "the tightest guy around," Theis demonstrated the depth of his commitment by buying a $500 accordion.

While Theis had had no formal music training, he believed he possessed the heritage to make music. Son of a German father and mostly Hispanic mother, young Theis was raised around the music of both cultures. His great grandfather Henry Beck used to lead a polka band at Schertz, Texas, and his ancestors were some of the original settlers of Anhalt, where Theis still returns for the Oktoberfest and Maifest dances.

Theis studied for a year with Fritz Morquecho, a master of the button accordion. Knowing that you never really learn an instrument until you play it with and for others, Theis started joining the jam session at the Longhorn Cafe in Harper every Friday evening.

"That jam has been going on over 20 years," he said. "Those guys are all strictly local, and learned it on the front porch. They play Czech, Mexican, and a little bit of German music. I was real fortunate to start with them and learn many styles."

For the past several months he has become confident enough to entertain passersby on Saturday afternoons.

"Their reactions are just wonderful," he said. "What I love is you always meet someone who was raised around it and wants to hear something special."

He didn't start street playing to make money, so he was surprised when people offered it.

"It's like–OK, throw the money in," he said, but added, "I didn't do this for the money in the slightest. I never dreamed of making money doing this. I feel like it is part of my culture, and I like to be for real."

Theis is so besotted with the instrument, he easily spends an hour a day playing.

"I always tell people that learning music takes a lot of discipline," he said. "The discipline is to put your instrument down and go out and make a real living."

"I can't say how gratifying this is. It's so much fun, it's unbelievable."
Aug 16, 2006

Jeryl Hoover: Words to act upon

I had the opportunity to appear in the Fredericksburg Theater Company's summer production of the *Wizard of Oz*. Truth be told, I was the tree. Actually, I was one of three trees. Comically, that is the apex of my acting ambition.

But even in my role of "scenery," I was privileged to observe how a theater production is put together. For those of us who were either out for sports or in the marching band in high school, and never had the opportunity to be in the school play, the camaraderie and learning and hard work that goes on behind the scenes is fascinating.

The most instructive part of theater work came during something called "everybody out." That is the time when everyone drops whatever they are doing and gathers around the director. The pre-rehearsal meeting gets everyone focused on what will be happening that night. The "post" is an often frank, but never brutal, analysis of what actually happened.

There we stood, some 90 of us–backstage crew and carpenters, kids and singers, bit players and leads, some in makeup, some half-costumed, but all concentrating on the words of Jeryl Hoover, Founder of FTC.

As I listened to Jeryl (who had no idea I would write this) it dawned on me that his words of advice and guidance had meaning beyond the edge of the stage. I began jotting down his observations. I thought it intriguing how advice for putting on a play could apply to life.

Take, for example, the daily meeting itself. Imagine how much more productive we might be if we started every activity with a focus meeting and ended it with an analysis.

Here are some of his statements. As you read them, think how they also apply to your work, your schooling, and your daily interactions with family and friends.

"Never turn your back to your audience."

"I look for people with enough self-awareness to know what they need to fix; and then care enough to fix it."

"Your only job is to create the illusion for the audience."

"Your job is to do your job."

"Shows really are just a series of 'moments' connected by other stuff."

"When acting, don't pretend to pretend. Pretend."

"I won't let you do less than your best."

"You don't decide where you go–go to your marks every time."

"Don't worry about what your feet are doing–worry about what your face is doing. That's where the audience will be looking."

"Your job is telling the story."

"Always be 'in the moment.'"

He said that last one a lot. After weeks of watching the witch fly in dozens of times, the Munchkins had a harder time pretending to be frightened. But the larger point is to consider in how many parts of our lives we fail to be "in the moment." We are thinking about what we will do later, or analyzing what has already happened, rather than absorbing the beauty and the moment that is unfolding in front of us.

Jeryl's final comments at the wrap party were about "acts of service." His point: words and promises mean little. All that counts are the "acts of service" one performs in helping the group accomplish its mission.

Having played a small part in a big play, I will watch future performances with a whole new understanding of what it means "to act."

Aug 1, 2007

Playing from the Heart

More personal reflections on music

Willie Nelson as Barbarosa, bronze by sculptor and washtub bass player Richard O. Cook. In the background is the bandanna I wore.

I Shot Willie Nelson (Part I)

I was perched on the low limb of a live oak tree. The sun was beginning to set behind me, casting long shadows over the sparse hill country brush. There was no sound, except for the cautious approach of footsteps on dry grass. A cedar limb moved slightly. Out stepped Willie Nelson, dressed in boots, leather chaps and vest, and wide brimmed sombrero. I knew it was Willie by his full red beard.

Barbarosa, I hissed between clenched teeth. I leveled the pistol through the leaves, sighting directly at the outlaw's heart.

"Cut!"

The action stopped. Willie leaned back and smiled.

"Thanks, Phil," the director said. "Okay, Danny, we are ready for you."

A crew member brought in a stepladder, and I climbed down from my perch. Danny De La Paz, the young actor who played Eduardo, walked over from behind the cameras and took my place. I sat in my folding chair and watched for the next hour as they shot and reshot the scene of "Eduardo" shooting Willie Nelson.

The year was 1980. I was passing through this cute little town of Fredericksburg, planning to play drums for a few weeks with my old friend Bill Smallwood. Around Thanksgiving the word went out that Willie Nelson would be in the area filming a new movie called *Barbarosa*, and they were looking for extras.

(Plot synopsis: Willie Nelson played a legendary outlaw, with Gary Busey as a young farmer who joins him, and both are on the run from a border family bent on revenge. Screenwriter was William Wittliff, who later worked on some obscure movies called *Lonesome Dove* and *The Perfect Storm*.)

Young, single, and with absolutely no direction in life, I headed out Tivydale Road along with half the residents of Gillespie County to be in a movie.

For several days I stood in horse pens and pretended to buy live-stock as Willie and Busey rode past over and over. I was an earnest actor, frowning, scratching my chin, and engaging in auction banter with the other amateur actors. (Turned out my acting was unnecessary, as not a bit of it appeared on screen.)

On what I thought was my final day of shooting, I was waiting to board the bus back to town. Smallwood caught me and said, "Hey, Phil... I overheard the director saying they were looking for a stand-in for Eduardo. You kinda look like him. Why don't you go over and talk to them?"

I had no idea what a stand-in was or what a stand-in did, but, being young, single, and with absolutely no direction in life, I tacked over to a group of people talking off to the side. I tapped a young man on the shoulder and announced, "I understand you are looking for a stand-in?"

The actor turned and slowly looked me up and down. I did the same to him. It was like Lucy and Harpo doing their "mirror" routine. Then he said to the director, "Fred, I think we've found him."

I was a dead ringer for De La Paz at the time. Same height, same build. We even had the same color curly hair and we both wore thin beards. He was supposed to be from Mexico, but I spoke as much Spanish as he did.

"Can you ride a horse?" the director asked. I said, "Si," and they hired me on the spot.

Next week, I'll tell you what a stand-in does.

And how Willie repaid me for shooting him.

March 18, 2009

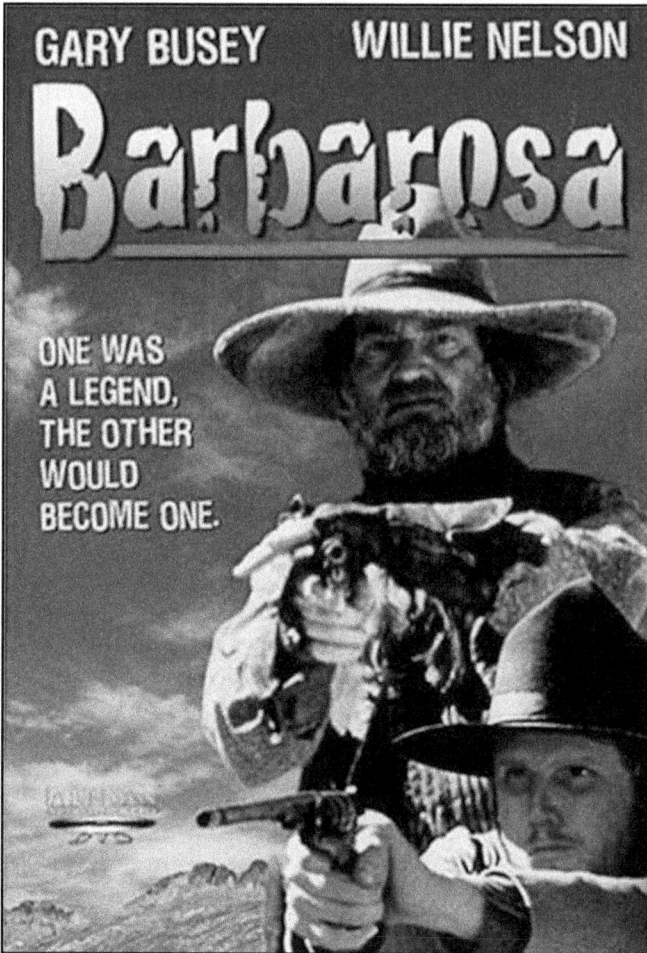

GARY BUSEY   WILLIE NELSON

Barbarosa

ONE WAS
A LEGEND,
THE OTHER
WOULD
BECOME ONE.

I Shot Willie Nelson (Part II)

*Note: Last week I wrote about my stint as an extra in the movie
Barbarosa, filmed around Fredericksburg in 1980 and starring Willie
Nelson and Gary Busey. On what was to be my last day on the set, the
film crew hired me as a stand-in for actor Danny De La Paz. Now, the
rest of the story...*

I soon learned what a movie stand-in did. For the next three weeks,
I simply "stood" in the spot where the actor would perform his scene.

The crew would nail down a small rubber "T" to show me where
to place my feet. I wore the exact same outfit as the actor. The crew
held a tape measure from my nose to the lens, then stuck a light meter
in front of my face. They even held up that "clapper" thing. It was
just like a scene from those corny skits where they pretend to make a

movie.

When every detail was set, the director (Fred Schepisi, who also directed *Six Degrees of Separation*) politely said, "Thank you, Phil," which was my cue to take a seat while the real actor acted.

Of course my big moment was crouching in the tree and "shooting" Willie Nelson as he emerged from the bushes. The director–thinking of protecting De La Paz from injury–considered filming me jumping from the tree and running away. That would have raised me to "stunt man" pay grade, but De La Paz insisted he could handle the action.

Lasting impressions from my stint on the Hollywood merry-go-round? Making movies is boring. Most of my 10-hour day was sitting in a director's chair while technicians set camera angles and focus, cleared brush, and scooped away horse manure. They even wrangled flies–can't have insects buzzing around movie stars and microphones.

They shot each scene over and over and over, from different angles and with different action and with different inflections. They were thrilled to get three minutes of usable footage a day.

My performance was hardly Oscar worthy. In fact, after a month on the set as an extra and a stand-in, my screen time was exactly zero minutes.

My friends were less than impressed. At the movie's premier, they quickly tired of hearing me say, "And in that scene I was sitting just off camera over there."

In the end I got no credits, no screen time. But I did have one especially memorable moment.

It was the final day of shooting, and we were at the base of Enchanted Rock. My actor had no scene on this day, but the director called me over. "Phil, would you mind lying down over here?"

I eased back on the hard granite, squirming to get comfortable. The director tucked several small blankets under my back, and kept asking if I was comfortable. When I finally said I was, a figure hovered over me and blocked out the Texas sun. A gloved hand appeared above me, which I clasped as I was pulled to my feet. I moved to the side, squinting to see who had helped me up.

It was Willie Nelson. "Thanks, Phil," he said, as he lied down in the spot I had prepared for him. Thank goodness he held no grudge from me trying to pop him off earlier in the week.

That was back in the days when Texas held the promise of being the next Hollywood, with its favorable tax and work laws, and a range of scenery from the coast to the piney woods to the llano estacado. But those dreams turned to tumbleweeds, as filmmakers fled to foreign lands like Louisiana and Michigan.

But I had my shot at a movie career. The studio held *Barbarosa* to a limited release, so it never played to a wide audience. After *Barbarosa*, my acting talents lay fallow for 30 years, until I was tapped as "man in bar" for a Fredericksburg Theater Company production.

There I was one of many, yet I knew that in that vast cast, I was the only one who had shot Willie Nelson.

March 25, 2009

Drum Lesson

The first time I played drums professionally, I was terrified.

I'd never been inside a tavern, much less sat behind a drum set on stage. With an audience. Well, with people sitting in the general area, talking, drinking, and smoking.

I was experiencing that indefinable gulf between practicing and performing.

Pounding drums in the basement to a Buck Owens record is existentially different than performing in a real band playing *Tiger by the Tail*. Even though you are technically going through the same motions, it's like the difference between singing in the shower and performing in Carnegie Hall.

So what did I do? I rushed. The adrenaline was churning so much that I took that beat and moved it along at an ever-increasing rate. The band–all veteran musicians–gallantly tried to hold me back. But I was so untested I did not realize I was rushing.

At the first break, the guitar player–Floyd–did a wise and wondrous thing, although I did not realize it until years later. As the rest of the band headed to the bar, Floyd set down his guitar and motioned me over to the side. He lit a cigarette, blew out the match, and gave me a conspiratorial wink. Drawing me close, he gestured to his brother Frank, who was ordering his Hamm's beer.

"Phil, you are doing a great job," he said, taking a deep puff. "But let me tell you a secret. That brother of mine? He's a good rhythm guitar player, but he rushes." He winked. "He can't help it, he always is speeding up the songs. What I want you to do next set is try to keep him steady." I listened and drank it all up, as serious as a 17-year-old farm boy at his first real gig could be. I nodded and set my jaw. I can do that, I reassured Floyd. "Good," he said. "And I want you to promise me something–Frank gets his feelings hurt, so don't tell him I told you this. Okay? Are you with me?"

We went on to a more relaxed rest of the gig. I worked diligently to "hold Frank back." I played with The Swingmasters for several more years. That gig grounded me in performing real country music, put me through college, and launched me on the road for several years performing across the country in show and lounge bands.

It was many years later, and I was back in Wellman, Iowa. Floyd, ever the wanderer, happened to be in town. Somehow Frank, Floyd, and I ended up playing for a party at a local farm to commemorate the end of harvest season.

At the break, we gathered around the keg and reminisced about those early years. The topic of my very first professional gig came up. Floyd grinned, then poked me and said, "Phil, do you remember what I told you that night?"

I smiled. "Of course. You said that Frank always rushed, so my job on the drums was to hold him back."

Floyd started laughing. "You know what?" he said. "Frank never rushed. I knew you were speeding up the songs, but I didn't want to crush you on your first night in a band. So I made up that story just so I wouldn't hurt your confidence."

I gazed at him in wonder and the dawning of understanding (I was still pretty naive).

Brother Frank, standing nearby, took this all in. He gave the classic slow turn and glared at Floyd. "You mean," he said, his voice rising in pitch with each measured word. "You mean you told him that I was rushing!" He set down his plastic cup, and took a deep breath. "Why, you no good, lying, son of a bitch, I ought to teach you a lesson right now."

But Floyd just laughed harder, leaning on the wall of the shed to keep from falling down. I started laughing, too.

Frank never did think it was funny.

I learned many things playing in the glow of neon beer signs. I learned to listen. I learned to relax while playing. I learned to improvise.

But it was a wise old guitar player who showed me how to handle people.

March 2, 2011

On the Road

Life on the road as a musician.

Ah. The travel, the sights. The fame, the fun.

It's all a myth.

I spent two years full time living the life of a road musician.

Hadn't thought much about it until a friend I hadn't heard from in 30 years called to reminisce about the travails of traveling cross country. These days, travel is not something I enjoy. Driving over two thousand miles to visit family is not an adventure to write home about. In fact, I'd rather write home than go home.

But back when I was 20, I had just finished two years of college and frankly was sick of going to school. I knew there was a fertile world beyond the farm fields of Iowa, and I was determined to dig in. So I loaded my drums into my pink 1962 Nash Rambler and headed west on Interstate 80.

Through a series of random circumstances (which may be another column), I met up with the Smallwoods in Fort Collins, Colorado.

For two years we crossed the country, playing six nights a week in lounges, clubs, bars, and the occasional county fair. For a kid who until then seldom left the county he was born in, it was a glorious adventure.

At first.

I remember pressing my nose to the windshield as I saw the skyline of Montgomery, of all places. Skiing the Ohio River. Learning that "barbecue" meant different things in Illinois, Kansas, and Georgia. Pitching songs on Music Row in Nashville. Playing for officers' wives in Officers Clubs. Playing for strippers in NCO clubs–clubs I was too young to get into if I was a customer.

Everywhere we went, people were warm and friendly. In places we played regularly, local families would invite us into their homes on weekends for food and fellowship. For this young fellow, some locals became too warm and friendly, and the six days came to an end at a propitious time. There were close calls in Shawneetown and Dodge City. Once I had to crawl out the back window of a motel.

Adventurous, yes. But it was not glamorous. Our sadistic agent would see how far he could make us drive between gigs. You know how many miles it is from Panama City, Florida, to Sault Sainte Marie, Michigan? Look it up.

We stayed in and played in motels and motor lodges. Some weeks we never left the complex, playing in the lounge, staying in the rooms upstairs, and eating in the dining rooms. Some places we rented cheap hotels by the week, with the band crowded into two rooms.

There were nights I slept in my car, waking up every hour to alternately lower the window to let in the air and rolling it up to keep out the mosquitoes.

I loved it.

But after weeks and months and years of playing on the road, something happened. We crossed paths with a band of older road musicians. They were probably in their 50s. We sat in a motel room before our respective gigs. They drank, played cards, told stories, and complained... of health issues, families disrupted, no retirement plan, car repairs, and club owners who didn't pay them.

I remember looking and listening that night, and having an epiphany: I don't want to be those men when I am their age.

It was shortly thereafter I returned to school and got my degree in education.

I played more music, for sure. In fact, playing on weekends was how I paid my way through the remaining two years of college. I still play to this day, though now it tends to be during daylight and within 20 minutes of home.

I don't regret one minute of my road experience (well, maybe the window thing). Would I do it again? Never.

Would I recommend it to a young musician?

Absolutely.

Jan 23, 2013

Phillips Sisters:
Heavenly Harmonies

On the banks of the Blanco River in 1980, I heard angels sing.

It was during an outing with the family of Les and June Phillips. While dating their daughter, I heard reference to the sisters being able to sing. But I had met many who inaccurately made that claim.

After lunch, I reclined on a picnic table bench for a nap. The sun warmed my skin, the river flowed, the breeze tickled.

As I drifted off, twin sisters Vickie and Valerie and younger sister Dawn gathered around me and began to sing. Deep in my dreams dawned a glorious sound. Clear melodies. Sinuous harmonies. A siren song roused me from slumber. I squinted my eyes; three faces were wreathed in light from the afternoon sun. This must be heaven, I thought, and they were angels.

Turns out the Phillips Sisters really could sing.

And they did sing at churches, clubs, and events. For many years they were featured on the gospel stage at the Texas Folklife Festival in San Antonio.

The Phillips Sisters sound is "sister harmony," that natural quality that blends like they were born to it, honed over years of singing in the Baptist church. I've tried analyzing it, but I can't. They break all the rules, taking turns singing high and low, sometimes switching parts in mid-phrase. Someone once had them sing back up on a studio recording. The producer carefully arranged vocal parts. The girls ignored the music. They did what they do best–sang the harmonies the way that felt right. It was exactly right.

My favorite thing is to watch the audience as the Phillips Sisters sing. When the girls do their opening piece a cappella, small talk stops. Forks pause, dominos drop, waiters wait. Just as I did on the riverbank, listeners find their own revelation.

I also love to watch the Phillips Sisters, because something magical happens.

"To me, it is euphoric," Vickie said. "Something comes over me that I can't describe. It is an inner peace, someplace I wish I could be all the time."

Valerie feels it. "It's the only time I am at peace and where I am not thinking about something else," she said. "It is total happiness, everything else just goes away."

Dawn feels it. "For me it's more of a spiritual connection," she said. "It's not about me getting away from the world, it's about forming a higher connection with the people around me. Doing something you love to do with people you love to do it with. Kind of like what heaven might be like."

I told you I heard angels.

Oct 15, 2008

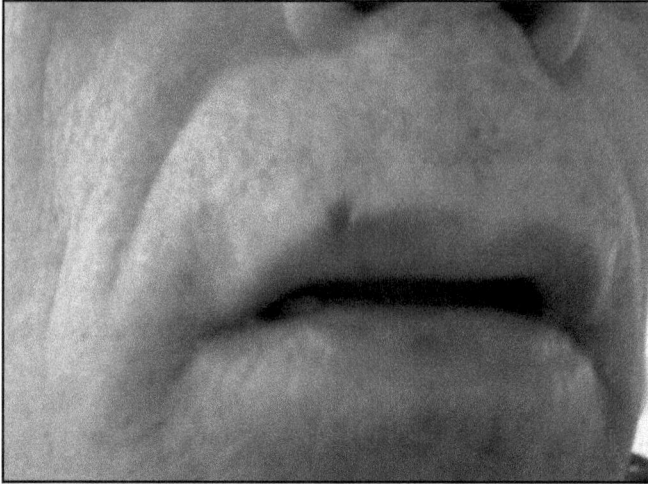

Punched

When I was asked to write an entertainment column, I never expected it would get me punched in the mouth.

But that is what happened on a Saturday in February while doing my usual rounds of Fredericksburg clubs, searching for ideas.

It had a been a pleasant evening, one of those times when camaraderie flowed, stories were exchanged, smiles smiled, wine sipped, and good music played.

I was decked out in my "reporter" garb, which has become a sort of visual trademark. I wore a suit and tie, suspenders, topped with a vintage grey hat from the Mad Men days. For the night, I had tucked a PRESS card in the hatband.

I stepped into a crowded club, tipped my hat as I passed two polite bouncers who nodded and checked me out. I was looking pretty dapper, I thought. I do as I always do–stand unobtrusively near a wall checking out the scene. I discretely scanned the room to see if there was anyone I knew. This night it was filled with strangers. The band was on break, so I decided to move on.

It was then that an acquaintance came up to me with a smile and a story. We chatted briefly, and I was about to ask a question, when it happened.

I caught a slight movement at the edge of my vision. I turned just in time to see a clenched fist coming at me. It connected to my upper right lip, snapping my head to the left. I fell back over a chair and caught a table.

Someone just hit me, I thought.

My reaction was interesting. I didn't feel anger, or fear, or surprise. It was more perplexity, as I tried to assess my situation. Here I was, speaking with a delightful lady, when a guy walked up and punched me.

I remember the feel of the knuckles on my lip. It was bone hard, not that "meat slap" you hear in movies. I experienced some of the slowdown in time, and also that feeling of detachment, as if this was happening to someone else.

The waitress brought me some bar napkins to catch the blood that was now dripping from my lip. Everyone was concerned for my well being, asking if I was all right. I was, surprisingly.

Who was it that hit me? I don't know. There was a bar full of witnesses, and no one knew him. I learned later that the man's companions hustled him down the street after the bouncers removed him from the club. All I remember is his face behind the fist, looking at me not as a person, but as an object, as if I were a plastic ficus.

I stepped outside and sat on the bench. I tried to process the experience as I held a bag of ice to my mouth. I just kept shaking my head and laughing.

I thought of all the novels I'd read where the hero gets punched. I always wondered how they know how to describe the sensation. Now, really for the first time in my life, I knew what it felt like to get punched in the mouth.

It feels much as I imagined it would. A numbness, the warm blood, the cold ice. The next day, a scab formed, and my front right incisor was still tender. There was some swelling.

Someone suggested pressing charges, but I wondered what would be the point. I had no malice. I only wanted to ask him why he did it.

Here is the saddest thing of all. As I staggered back from the punch, my very first thought was, "I wonder if I could get a column out of this."

I did.

March 13, 2013

Recital Time

It's May, which means it is time for young and old to gather into groups to witness that enduring rite of spring: the recital.

I was introduced to this ritual under the metronome of Mrs. Gardner, a kind lady who taught me and my eight brothers and sisters to play piano.

Every May we would meet at the local Methodist church (why are recitals always held in Methodist churches?) to show off another year of progress on our musical journey toward becoming accountants, coaches, and insurance salesmen.

I remember my first recital piece: *The Wise Old Owl*. I can still play it by heart. And I still remember the stark terror leading up to the actual performance. I endured the weekly piano lessons. I endured the oppression of practicing seven or eight minutes every day. And on the evening of the performance I endured the cruelty of washing my face and wearing a bow tie.

I remember waiting my turn sitting on those cold folding chairs, digging fingers into thighs trapped inside black polyester pants. I remember hearing my name called. I remember standing up and walking to the front of that room full of staring adults.

But I can't for the life of me remember actually playing the piece.

I now know that my first recital was not the most terrifying experience in my life. No–it would be topped in sheer terror many years later by... BEING THE PARENT OF KIDS WHO HAVE RECITALS.

For over 25 years my wife and I have watched our children solo in dance, singing, piano, and violin. We are now on our fourth kid, and let me assure you young parents it never gets easier.

But I do have the advantage of perspective. I can sit back and have as much fun watching the audience as I do listening to the performers. Even in a Methodist church full of strangers, you can always tell whose kid is on stage. They are the couple that strain forward in their seats, neck veins bulging, cheeks flushed, and nails clawing into their thighs through black polyester pants.

The best outcome for these parents is having their prodigy get clean through the song without missing more than three notes. The absolute nightmare is... the pregnant pause. That is when the earnest student–who has undoubtedly worked many weeks to memorize the piece–freezes up. It happens at least once at every recital. Ditty-ditty-dum-dum they go along, then... silence. Silence in a church full of people is like darkness in a cave–it becomes a suffocating specter hanging from the flying buttresses. The parents stop breathing, the accompanist poises to jump to where the student goes, and the teacher smiles and pretends this is normal.

But the reluctant star of the pause is always the student. The sacrificial innocent stares into the ether, certain the next note will show its face from the choir loft. Parents squirm, grandparents wake up, little brothers stop poking little sisters. Slowly, mercifully, the student recovers, fingers start to move, the piece continues. The recital is saved!

I know there are benefits of the recital experience. It teaches confidence and builds character. But maybe we could reinvent the recital into something like a Luckenbach jam session, where players sit in a circle and take turns leading the song. I know having access to alcohol would help.

But as long as there are music students and music teachers, there will be music recitals. And someday my grandkids will be playing.

I'll be there... clutching my thighs.

May 4, 2011

Bob and Maxine Houseal,
a young couple who first found each other on the dance floor.

Dance

Everyone should dance.

I'm not in the habit of handing out advice to my children. First, I don't have any advice. Second, if I did, they wouldn't take it. I never did.

But when my oldest son set off for college, I felt I should say something profound. So I told him this: Take a ballroom dance class.

He simply raised an eyebrow.

In spite of providing him material he could have a good laugh over when he told his future children stupid things his dad said, there was logic to my statement.

I believe everyone should dance. As a musician, writer, and observer of people, I have noticed few things make people stand out in the real world of business and personal life like the ability to dance.

If you are a man, especially.

At formal social occasions, the man who is light on his feet is a sought after partner. A man who is comfortable doing the foxtrot is comfortable making a sales call or speaking in front of groups. And I believe that how a couple moves together on the dance floor is a screening process for finding possible mates.

My parents were both good dancers. Thank God. If they weren't, I wouldn't be here. My mom recently told me the story of the night she met my dad.

It was in 1942, and there was a community dance in the small Iowa town of Keota. My then teenaged mom (Maxine) was sent to the dance hall to pick up her younger sister. When she walked into the dance, something magical happened.

"There stood a sailor," she told me. Now, Keota, Iowa, is pretty landlocked, if you don't count the North Fork of the Skunk River. Having a sailor in town caused quite a ripple among the marriageable girls. Maxine remembers the moment distinctly, even what she was wearing–a brown jumper with a sweater. Not that it mattered. "He was staring at me. I felt like I didn't have any clothes on."

She learned later that he was looking to see if she had on a wedding ring. At least that's what he told her. Dad, you scoundrel.

That sailor (Bob, and by now you know he was also my future father), asked Maxine to dance. She finally gave in. That's how she told it, anyway.

Maxine was in heaven. "The other girls came up to me and said, 'How do you rate?' There was only one sailor there, and he asked me to dance."

And dad could dance. They did the jitterbug, the lindy hop, the foxtrot, swing, and all the hot dances of the 40s. Something clicked, because they danced a lot more, married, had nine kids, and stayed married.

Even growing up, I remember them going out dancing every Saturday night. They belonged to a square dance club, and sometimes they took us kids with them. Dad taught the jitterbug to my sisters. There was always music, and always movement. He would even invite the neighbors over for old-fashioned barn dances with a live caller.

So perhaps it is no surprise that I was fascinated by dancing. While in high school and college, I discretely took every dance class I could, from ballroom and folk dancing to jazz and ballet. I talked my younger brother Mike into taking tap lessons in someone's basement. I convinced a group of my college classmates to join the local square dance club. This was in the 1970s, and I'm still not sure which group was more surprised–the long-haired college kids or the blue-haired square dancers. But it worked; we made friends and had fun.

When I eventually joined a band and passed through the Texas town of Fredericksburg, I was that rarity in the music world–a drummer that could dance. At Pat's Hall one night I spied a little red-haired girl, whose parents had apparently taught her to dance, too. After protracted staring, I didn't find any wedding ring either. So I asked her to dance. That two-step led to four kids and 30-plus years of marriage so far.

A few weeks into my son's first semester at college, he called and was going over his schedule. Then he lowered his voice and almost whispered into the phone, "I got into a ballroom dance class."

Ah, the circle of life. Who knows if it will affect his future as drastically as it did for my parents and for me. If nothing else, it will make parties more interesting.

And give him an excuse to stare at that cute girl waiting by the edge of the dance floor.

June 5, 2013

www.ingramcontent.com/pod-product-compliance
Lightning Source LLC
Chambersburg PA
CBHW052008090426
42741CB00008B/1596